Praise for **The Right Kind of White**

"I am so grateful to Garrett Bucks for his words, his wisdom, his wit, and most of all his willingness to thoroughly excavate his whiteness, his male-ness, and his good-ness. *The Right Kind of White* is a deeply revealing and vulnerable memoir that manages to be the opposite of navel-gazing—it's personal narrative for the greater good, self-knowledge-as-activism, and a compelling critique of the holier-than-thou mindset that us 'good' white people engage in. I rarely read or recommend books by straight white dudes, but this one is a truly exceptional exception. Thank you, Garrett."

—Kate Schatz, *New York Times* bestselling co-author of
Do the Work: An Antiracist Activity Book
and the *Rad Women* book series

"*The Right Kind of White* is a brilliant, unsparing memoir about the dreamworld of white American liberalism, where good intentions often mask the origins and consequences of white supremacy. Garrett Bucks has been to all every stop on the tour—liberal arts colleges, Methodist church basements, even Teach for America—and he's here to tell us how hard, and necessary, it is for 'good white people' to confront hard truths about themselves."

—Jess Row, author of *White Flights*

"Things get tricky when someone wants to do good—and also be celebrated for it. Garrett Bucks offers a fascinating, immersive account of what it means to be white and progressive in a time of social and political reckoning. *The Right Kind of White* is unforgettable. It's an elegant testament to the pitfalls of ego and the desire for absolution."

—Wendy S. Walters, author of *Multiply/Divide*

"Garrett Bucks's *The Right Kind Of White* is a clear-eyed, deeply felt call for connection and community rather than individual saviorism. Bucks invites us to follow his path from a progressive childhood into a commitment to social justice work that hinged on exalting his separation from other white people. Recognizing this tendency writ large in white activist circles, Buck argues that the only way to reckon with whiteness and its harms is to give up trying to stand outside them, but to do the work for change together with other white people in a spirit of love rather condemnation."

—Maud Newton, author of *Ancestor Trouble*

"It's easy to mistake self-flagellation for introspection. And it's much easier to perform that self-flagellation for others—and mistake that performance for actually doing the work of dismantling white privilege. Garrett Bucks has done both, and he knows it. But he also knows that there can be a different way forward: a way of grappling with whiteness in which the primary concern is not self-absolution. That's the beating heart of *The Right Kind of White,* a must-read for anyone who's ready to *actually* do the work."

—Anne Helen Peterson, author of *Can't Even*

"*The Right Kind of White* is a funny, honest, beautiful, and necessary hard look at race, community, and belonging in America. Beginning with his own sense of self and identity, Garrett Bucks flips around notions of do-gooder liberalism and asks hard questions about community race and belonging in America. This book is important reading for all well-meaning White people who want to do better and build better communities. Garrett has written an indispensable manual to understanding ourselves and our communities and how we belong and how we can make them better."

—Lyz Lenz, author of *This American Ex-Wife*

"*The Right Kind of White* could be called *The Right Kind of Masculinity* or *The Right Kind of Middle Class Progressive*, which is to say, it's a sneak attack examination on the ways in which we often play to our roles rather than living into our deepest, least constructed knowing about love and justice. Garrett tells a familiar story—white do-gooder coming of age—in a completely fresh and surprising way. Dude sees the way that his choices have been led by exceptionalism fantasy and tries to come back down to the messy, beautiful Earth. Full of tenderness, humor, and aching toward a collective mindset, this book is sure to lead so many others down a path of joyful self-examination."

—Courtney E. Martin, author of *Learning in Public* and *The New Better Off*

The Right Kind of White

Garrett Bucks

SIMON & SCHUSTER PAPERBACKS
New York   Amsterdam/Antwerp   London
Toronto   Sydney/Melbourne   New Delhi

Simon & Schuster Paperbacks
An Imprint of Simon & Schuster, LLC
1230 Avenue of the Americas
New York, NY 10020

First Simon & Schuster trade paperback edition March 2025

SIMON & SCHUSTER PAPERBACKS and colophon are registered
trademarks of Simon & Schuster, LLC.

Simon & Schuster strongly believes in freedom of expression
and stands against censorship in all its forms.
For more information, visit BooksBelong.com.

For information about special discounts for bulk purchases,
please contact Simon & Schuster Special Sales at
1-866-506-1949 or business@simonandschuster.com.

The Simon & Schuster Speakers Bureau can bring authors to
your live event. For more information or to book an event, contact
the Simon & Schuster Speakers Bureau at 1-866-248-3049
or visit our website at www.simonspeakers.com.

Interior design by Lewelin Polanco

Manufactured in the United States of America

1 3 5 7 9 10 8 6 4 2

Library of Congress Cataloging-in-Publication Data has been applied for.

ISBN 978-1-9821-9720-9
ISBN 978-1-9821-9721-6 (pbk)
ISBN 978-1-9821-9722-3 (ebook)

For Evelyn, George, Vera, and Russell

Notes from the Author

In the spirit of telling my own story (and not presuming to tell any stories other than my own), I've used pseudonyms throughout the text. The only exceptions are for public figures, my immediate family members, and a few close family friends. To all the friends, colleagues, students, and acquaintances who are in this book in anonymized form, thank you for being a part of my life. To all the Bucks and Gelston family members reading this, as well as Kjersti, Olof, and Ida, I love you all so much, and I sincerely hope I did right by our shared stories.

Throughout the text, I've done my best to recount scenes and conversations from my past (including direct quotes) as accurately as possible. Obviously, this is a deeply imperfect exercise, especially the further back I went in my history. Thank you to all readers for your grace with the imperfection of recollection and perspective.

Finally, I chose to capitalize all ethnic and racial designations throughout the text, including the words "Black" and "White." I was influenced in this choice both by the White journalist Courtney E. Martin and the Black sociologist Eve L.

Ewing. In her essay "I'm a Black Scholar Who Studies Race. Here's Why I Capitalize 'White,'" Ewing writes that when the word "White" is not capitalized, it gives the impression that White people are "normal, neutral, or without any race at all, while the rest of us are saddled with this unpleasant business of being racialized." Given that this text explores my relationship to other White people—both as individuals and as a collective—that stylistic choice felt particularly important.

Introduction

I have often wondered, and it is not a pleasant wonder, just what white Americans talk about with one another.
—JAMES BALDWIN, "THE WHITE MAN'S GUILT"

I first heard "Rednecks," Randy Newman's 1974 "pox on both your houses" song about American Whiteness, in Stockholm, Sweden. It was the fall of 2006. Thanks both to the largesse of an extremely low-accountability government research scholarship and a quirk in Stockholm University's wireless internet network that enabled me to listen to other students' iTunes music libraries, it was an incredible year for music discovery, if not for progress on my ostensible research project.

"Rednecks" is told from the perspective of an unnamed southern good old boy. Its narrator is spoiling for a fight, having just witnessed former Georgia governor Lester Maddox's infamous 1970 appearance on *The Dick Cavett Show*. Maddox, a chicken shop owner turned segregationist politician, rose to fame for literally chasing Black patrons away from his establishment with a meat cleaver. His interview with Cavett was a disaster. Sitting next to Jim Brown, the famous Black football star, Maddox exploded when faced with a question about whether his supporters were bigots. For more than three minutes of airtime, Maddox huffed, puffed, and demanded various apologies before storming off the set. It made for great television. The audience gasped and howled as Maddox played into every stereotype of a bloviating, racist White southern villain.

The narrator in "Rednecks" doesn't really defend Maddox and his fellow southerners. Unlike the governor, he's proud of his bigotry. The n-word glides from his lips with ease. He speaks openly about how he and his compatriots keep Black people down. It isn't Cavett's accusation that offends him. It's the host's smugness, his assumption that he (a "smart-ass New York Jew," per the narrator, inaccurately) is somehow above the fray.

To the tune of Newman's jaunty Dixieland piano, the narrator makes his case. How different, he argues, is the old Dixie segregation in Georgia from the "cage" that Blacks are "put" into in northern cities like Boston and Chicago and San Francisco?

I listened to "Rednecks" on cheap headphones at an institutional metal table in Stockholm University's student union, simultaneously impressed with Newman's trenchant observations and my ability to agree with them. *That's right! All White people are racist! In both the North and the South!* I got it. More important, I assumed there were other White people who didn't get it. That distinction mattered to me. The song was a test, and I had aced it.

For nearly fifteen years after that first listen, I didn't seek out "Rednecks." When Newman's song popped up on some algorithmically generated playlist in 2020, as a spring of lockdowns and isolation gave way to a summer of street uprisings and competing yard signs in White neighborhoods (BLACK LIVES MATTER VS. BACK THE BADGE), I heard it with new ears. This time, I was less interested in the song's moral than I was in its characters, especially those characters' obsession with each other. I noticed the good old boy narrator again. Not the fact of his bigotry, which wasn't surprising, but the fact that he couldn't stop thinking about all those hypocritical northern Whites who must be judging him.

The narrator isn't wrong that he's being judged. Just as he's obsessed with Cavett and his refined Yankee audience, so too are they obsessed with him and his fellow rednecks. The proof is right there on the screen, in Maddox's appearance on Cavett's talk show. The narrator may be fictional, but the exchange between the governor and the TV host really happened. Cavett never challenges Maddox on his record; he's surprisingly complimentary on that front. His critiques are all about the unseen masses that Maddox presumably represents. He keeps coming back to the question. He needs Maddox to admit that Georgia is home to bigots and that those bigots love their governor.

———

This isn't a book about the core message of "Rednecks," about how there are no "good" or "bad" White people, about how all White people are complicit in the maintenance of White supremacy. There is no shortage of books that make that case, from classics like James Baldwin's *The Fire Next Time* and Frantz Fanon's *Black Skin, White Masks* to contemporary bestsellers like Isabel Wilkerson's *Caste* and Robin DiAngelo's *White Fragility*.

What has often gone underexplored—particularly by White writers—is the story between the lines of Newman's song, the story of White people's obsession not just with who we are in relation to Black and Brown people, but who we are in relation to each other.

There's an argument to be made that if we're interested in ending racism and other systems of domination, there's no point in focusing on White identity. After all, Whiteness is an invented concept, a grab-bag into which various ethnic groups were assimilated for the purpose of establishing and maintaining capitalist hierarchies. But merely saying "Whiteness is imaginary" doesn't make the hundreds-year-old story of Whiteness disappear; that narrative is now embedded in millions of family trees. There can be no transformation of Whiteness without an honest examination of it from a variety of angles, including the question of how Whiteness reacts when it sees itself in the mirror.

This book seeks to tell a single White story: my own. It is an accounting of the ways, throughout my life, that I attempted to define my Whiteness in relation and reaction to other White people. I have spent decades operating as though Whiteness was a moral stain I could cleanse myself of if only I performed a certain set of rituals. I looked on other White people, especially White men, with suspicion. I have worried, implicitly if not explicitly, that if I didn't successfully distinguish myself from every other White person around me, that I'd be stained by their less palatable Whiteness.

In short, I've obsessed over being "the right kind of White," which is to say, with the notion that I could somehow outrun everything uncomfortable about White identity—the weight of history, the worry that my accomplishments have not been fully earned, the guilt of a lifetime of mistakes and harm—by first separating myself from other White people.

I don't pretend that my particular version of being "the right kind of White" is universal. My attempts at self-justification have been shaped not just by my Whiteness, but by my family's left-liberal politics, my midwestern and western roots, my class and educational background, my gender and sexual orientation, the relative lack of trauma I've experienced, and the particular era of American history in which I came of age. There are so many other versions of "the right kind of White": the color-blind White, the Make America Great Again White, the "I don't think about politics" White, the White feminist, the White antifeminist, the White person who only hangs out with people of color. Our stories are different, but we are all storytellers.

I originally conceived of this book as a sociohistorical analysis of the varying ways that White people have defined themselves in relation to one another throughout American history. I realized very early in that process, though, that while I truly believe that there's a collective narrative at play here, I couldn't honestly tell that story without first interrogating my own. Furthermore, I challenged myself to root the text solely in the last few generations of my family's story—long after both branches of my family tree were assimilated into Whiteness. That's not to downplay the power of pre-assimilation stories, particularly for White ethnic communities for whom assimilation has been more recent, but it is an acknowledgment of the current task at hand. I am, for better or worse, fully White, and that is the racial reality with which I must personally wrestle.

Writing this book has been terrifying and powerful. It's a gift to share my story of "the right kind of being White." It will be an even more profound gift if my doing so encourages others to share theirs as well.

The
Right
Kind of
White

PART ONE

Origin
Story

Chapter ONE

The dog-eared worksheet in my lap read "When did you first discover that you were _____?" but since I had dutifully followed our facilitator's instructions and scrawled in my answer, the question now read "When did you first discover that you were <u>WHITE</u>?"

If I'm remembering correctly, it was winter, early 2001, my sophomore year of college. I was nineteen years old and already incredibly skilled at filling in blanks. Those little black lines with the negative space above them meant that this was an exercise with right or wrong answers.

There were about twelve to fourteen of us gathered that Saturday midmorning on the faded, mismatched couches of Stout Meetinghouse's second-floor library. We were all Peace and Global Studies majors, which meant that we were the most self-consciously earnest do-gooders at Earlham College, a Quaker school on the eastern edge of Indiana that primarily attracted self-consciously earnest do-gooders.

Our clothing was thrifted and ill fitting, communicating, we hoped, the half-truth (at best) that we possessed neither disposable income nor self-consciousness about our appearance. We carried Nalgene water bottles stickered with tributes to the Grateful Dead and Black Flag, Yosemite and Yellowstone National Parks, and various idealistic political concerns: NO NUKES! BUSH AND GORE MAKE ME WANT TO RALPH: VOTE NADER 2000. IT WILL BE A GREAT DAY WHEN OUR SCHOOLS GET ALL THE MONEY THEY NEED AND THE AIR FORCE HAS TO HOLD A BAKE SALE TO BUY A BOMBER. We didn't complain when we learned that we were to attend this weekend retreat together; to us, nonviolent social change wasn't just a nice idea, it was something to learn and to master.

The whole retreat wasn't devoted to diversity training. There were get-to-know-you games and planning meetings (though I can't for the life of me remember what we were planning together) and a potluck where we shared the handful of vegetarian entrées that could be reasonably assembled in a dorm kitchen: Black Bean Enchiladas of Sorts, Vegetable Korma That Means Well, Tex-Mex Chili With Tofu For Some Reason. The diversity training was a clear centerpiece, though. Its prominence in the weekend's schedule was a clue that we were to take it—both racial justice as a general concept as well as this specific question about when we first discovered our racial identity—quite seriously.

On our way to the meetinghouse that morning, we walked past a dour-looking statue of a colonial-era woman in a long dress and a headscarf. The inscription on its base read:

MARY DYER

QUAKER

WITNESS FOR RELIGIOUS FREEDOM

HANGED ON BOSTON COMMON—1660

It was an accurate and succinct telling of the Mary Dyer story: she was a Quaker in Puritan Massachusetts, and because she was unwilling to renounce her then radical religion, that colony's governor ordered her hanging. Both serene and full of righteous conviction, the stone martyr's eyes lent an extra layer of purpose to the meetinghouse gatherings. *I literally died for you, you know!* Mary Dyer reminded us from her solid rectangular pillar. *I don't care if some of you are hungover or if some of you would rather be playing video games! I was a Quaker! And they killed me for it! Don't mess this up!*

Scared straight by a long-dead Yankee colonist, we tried our best. We filled in the blank with our racial identity. All but three of us wrote "White." We then sat in Quakerly silence to consider the second part of the question: when we first discovered what race we were. Many of my peers wrote feverishly, filling both the worksheet and additional notebooks with scribbled reflections. I mostly added deeper and deeper layers of wrinkles to my own sheet of paper, a nervous habit. I already knew what I wanted to say.

When it came time to share, we went around the circle clockwise. I did my best not merely to listen but to show just how *hard* I listened to my classmates' stories. This was a crucial skill in leftist workshop attendance. It required near but not total silence, so I let out a few soulful sighs. Not too loud, but audible. I nodded my head, but not too vigorously. I made eye contact, but I also knew when to close my eyes as if I had been knocked into sudden meditative reflection by the sheer force of a classmate's wisdom.

Because this was a workshop about racial justice, I had to listen particularly well to my classmates of color. When Tim, a South Asian Alaskan, talked about being alone in a sea of Whiteness, I nodded. When Fatima, from Iraq, related the many times when she had been accused of being a terrorist, I sighed disapprovingly. I felt both relieved and ashamed of my relief that my friend Jay, who was biracial and who organized Black students on campus, hadn't been able to make it that morning. At a different workshop, Jay had taken an unnamed group of White activists to task for criticizing a "Day of Silence" by students of color as being politically counterproductive. I had been one of the White students who expressed concerns, and when Jay issued his critique, I could have sworn he was staring at me.

Listening to the other White students was so much easier. There was nothing to feel guilty or defensive about in their stories. There also weren't any surprises. When it was our turn to talk, we all sighed our contemplative sighs, directed our gaze at the worn midcentury rug in the center of the room, and then took our turn sharing what was, with slight variations, basically the same story.

In other spaces, I would have felt embarrassed at the similarity between all the other White stories and my own. I would have sought to put a special twist on my narrative that would move the room to a spontaneous standing ovation. But today was about checking a very specific set of boxes.

Plus, there was the matter of who else was in the room. These were the people I had spent my whole life trying to find: Shaggy leftists. The sons and daughters of public school teachers and librarians. The only kids from our respective high schools with an interest in composting. We had all found our way here, to an obscure liberal arts college with a hard-to-pronounce name, precisely because it offered majors like Peace and Global Studies.

Most of us were not Quakers, but we came here for the vague promise of what a Quaker education offered: humility, social justice, and community. We were twentysomethings who hoped that our college experience might somehow deliver us from the horrors of an unjust world.

When I say that I wanted to ensure that my reply mirrored that of my classmates, I wasn't playacting, at least not consciously. It's just that I knew there was a right answer, one that would elicit a maximum number of nods and "hmms" from the audience. I knew my story wasn't supposed to be about deep internal reflection. It had to be about my first conscious encounter with somebody who wasn't White. It had to be a collision story—in my case, quite literally.

My version of our shared "how I discovered I was White" story took place at St. Paul's United Methodist Church in Helena, Montana. Helena is an old mining town that became a government town when it was named the capital of

Montana Territory in 1875. Its central business district sits in a cavern-like gulch protected by steep hills on both sides. St. Paul's is on one of those hills. Helena is much more Catholic than it is Methodist, and St. Paul's is just down the street from the towering Cathedral of Saint Helena, a true citadel of a building—the closest thing to a skyscraper for hundreds of miles. St. Paul's building wasn't a shack, but it wasn't magisterial. It was a nondescript, replacement-level frontier sanctuary. My family lived a half hour away from both churches, just outside a tiny former mining outpost called Clancy.

Even though the Helena Methodists didn't have the most impressive building on the block, my parents taught us that we should feel fortunate to get to make the trip once a week. Members of our church were in a political satire/social justice–y folk band. They were friends with Archbishop Desmond Tutu, the South African theologian known for his work as an anti-apartheid and human rights activist, who adored them so much that he invited them to perform with him on numerous occasions. I didn't know who Desmond Tutu was nor why he mattered, but if he was famous that meant that our modest Montana church must be an important place.

My Whiteness recognition story was straightforward. I was six. Sunday school had just finished for the day. I bounded down the steps to the fellowship hall as quickly as possible. The stairwells at St. Paul's were narrow and twisting, with blind corners, which meant that my perenially frightened six-year-old cannonball of a body presented a clear danger to anybody attempting to come up the steps. So when I collided into the first Black man I ever remember seeing in person, I don't remember if he said anything or if I apologized. I just recall picking myself up and sprinting to my parents with a story to tell.

"I just saw somebody new in the stairwell."

Even though I didn't tell her that I had seen a Black person, my mom immediately knew who I was talking about. There had only been one Black man in the sanctuary that day, a friendly but anonymous visitor. She beamed at me and offered that I had just run into a very nice man.

Had I stopped to consider this story, I would have noticed how anomalous it was from all the other moments when I first understood an aspect of my identity.

I understood I was a boy (and what it meant to be a boy) in our basement in Clancy—somewhere around age four or five—watching TV commercials on Saturday morning, paying more attention to them than my parents would have liked. The commercials with boys in them were for Transformers and G.I. Joes. A mélange of noise, steel, explosions, and guns. I never convinced my pacifist parents to purchase one of the trucks that turns into a gun-wielding robot for me, but I knew from the boys in the commercial that I was at least supposed to try.

I understood I was my parents' biological child when I was three or four years old and my mother signed us up to be a foster family. Soon our house was filled with babies who were not my siblings but whom I was to care for as if they were my siblings. One of those babies would join our family permanently—my sister, Anna, my closest sibling in age. Anna would always announce that she was adopted, a distinction that meant I wasn't adopted.

I understood I was straight when I was in fourth grade. I knew I wanted to date Allison Gomez. I was friends with a lot of boys and girls, but I didn't want to date any of my male friends. I wanted to date girls—first Allison Gomez, then so many others.

I understood that something about the combination of liking girls and being a boy meant that I wasn't supposed to cross my legs. Riding the Metro in Washington, D.C., with my family, my brothers saw me place one leg over the other in a diagonal slant. "That's not how guys sit," I remember them saying. I uncrossed my legs.

I understood I was German when my brothers Eric and Brian won scholarships to study abroad in Schleswig-Holstein, Germany. Eric and Brian look like my mother, who is of Irish descent, but when their host families saw a picture of me, my brother Nate, and my dad, they swore up and down that we looked like every one of their neighbors.

I understood I was Irish because my mother served us corned beef and cabbage on Saint Patrick's Day and regaled us with stories of British misdeeds.

Each of those discoveries taught me either about myself or how the world viewed me. That wasn't the case for the stories that we earnest young White do-gooders shared in that circle, though. We pretended that they were stories about us, but they were really about the person we noticed. We noticed the woman in the hijab dressed differently from how our moms dressed. We noticed the waiters in a restaurant speaking a language that we and our families didn't speak. We noticed that the Black man in the stairwell looked different from us and the other parishoners at St. Paul's.

Two decades later, when Donald Trump was president, Black Lives Matter was an active point of debate, and talking and writing about Whiteness was my full-time job, I read Toni Morrison's *Playing in the Dark: Whiteness and the Literary Imagination*, a collection of lectures Morrison delivered about the way that Blackness shows up in the White American literary canon. It was the first time I actually had language for the stories that White people tell in circles like that one.

Morrison argued that throughout the history of White literature (she specifically cites works by Willa Cather, Edgar Allan Poe, and Ernest Hemingway), Blackness (which she refers to as "the Africanist presence") appears as the shadow, the contrast by which Whiteness knows not what it is but what it is not. "Africanism," according to Morrison, "is the vehicle by which the [White] American self knows itself as not enslaved, but free; not repulsive, but desirable; not helpless, but licensed and powerful; not history-less, but historical; not damned, but innocent."

Put differently, while each of us around that circle claimed that we were sharing the moment we discovered our Whiteness, we actually shared a moment when the presumed defaultness of our racial identity was called into question, if only for a second. We noticed somebody else's lack of Whiteness. We noticed that they were *not the norm*, that their presence in our hero's journey was unexpected. We noticed that their appearance in our lives made us feel something about ourselves, but we didn't say what. Not in that circle. Nor ever, really.

What we were really saying was that we never actually noticed ourselves as White. One minute, we noticed ourselves as normal, because everybody around us was like us. And then, in the moment of puncture, the moment somebody Black or Brown appeared in frame, we didn't feel White. We felt exposed.

Chapter TWO

I hoped that everybody around that meetinghouse circle—the people of color especially—understood that I was the kind of White boy who did not judge the Black man into whom I collided. I'm not sure if I successfully landed that rhetorical plane, mind you. I pointedly knew nothing about that man, not even his name. The only thing I had going for me was that I didn't actively blame him for having the temerity to be run into. What I could express, though, was my obvious pride in my mother's reaction to the news. That mattered. I wanted everybody to believe how thoughtful and not racist I was, but I *really* wanted them to know that my freedom from prejudice and hate was, in fact, a family legacy.

My father, Dan Bucks, grew up on his family's farm in what is now Bettendorf, Iowa. While today Bettendorf has grown large enough to be considered the fifth of the inaccurately named Quad Cities, back when that town was much smaller, Davenport was the city that eastern Iowan families drove to in order to birth their babies, furnish their homes, and haggle with the bank.

One day, in the early 1950s, my father, his older brother, Dale, and his younger sister, Karen, were walking with their parents down Davenport's Main Street when they saw a Black family for the first time. My father was roughly the same age as I was in my St. Paul's story. Karen didn't notice the family, but the two boys turned their heads and gawked. My grandfather Russell Bucks stopped in his tracks. He wasn't one for bold pronouncements, but he made an exception this time. My father remembered his message clearly.

"Boys, those people are just like us. There are people who don't believe that they are—that want to treat them badly. But those people are wrong."

A few years later, Russell took Dan and Dale with him to the big livestock show at the Chicago stockyards. Typically, rural White farmers dropped their cattle off for sale but otherwise gave the Black neighborhoods around the stockyards a wide berth. My father noticed that my grandfather hung around, eating in Black restaurants, staying at a Black hotel, and getting his hair cut at a Black barbershop. Russell didn't say anything to his sons about those choices, but my father suspected there was a message there as well.

That statement in Davenport. Those decisions in Chicago. My grandparents' general quiet kindness and loyalty to prairie populist politicians. Those were the bread crumbs that guided my father to understand what kind of White people his parents were, and therefore what kind of White person he should be. He had no idea how either my grandfather, who had left school after eighth grade, or my grandmother Vera, who graduated high school but never left eastern Iowa, developed such progressive racial views. Neither parent talked openly about their social beliefs, but the message, from both Russell's short lectures and Vera's nodded assent, was clear. There were even rumors that their convictions may have played a role in their departure from Iowa. His parents never shared the full story, but the whispers were that they had been squeezed out by a cousin who was active in the arch-conservative John Birch Society, forcing them to arrange a farm trade with a distant relative in South Dakota.

Russell and Vera's second farm was outside the town of Doland. They moved just as my father started high school. A serious young man who did not want to be mistaken for a dumb farm boy, Dan Bucks arrived at Doland High School with a briefcase. On his first day at Doland High, my mother hid it from him—a not-so-subtle message that Dolandites weren't impressed by puffed-up signifiers of intellectual superiority.

The second-oldest child of Evelyn and George Gelston, my mother, Jane, spent her whole life in Doland. My grandmother Evelyn was originally from Mitchell, a big town by South Dakota standards, nearly ten thousand residents strong and home to the famous corn palace. She was a smart girl with equally smart siblings. After finishing high school, she completed a two-year teaching degree from Dakota Wesleyan University, the respectable Methodist school in town.

Evelyn's sister, Ethel, married an engineer and moved to Southern California. Evelyn stayed in South Dakota, took a teaching job in Doland, and met a fuel truck driver named George Gelston, who very much loved being a fuel truck driver from Doland. My grandmother wished that her and her sister's roles were reversed. But they weren't, so the girl who dreamed beyond the prairie and the boy who was quite happy there stayed put in his hometown. George joined the fire brigade, befriended the farmers on his route, and went pheasant hunting in the fall. Evelyn helped fundraise for the town library and sustained the Doland women's literary society.

My mom grew up just a block or so away from Main Street, home to both her mother's library and the Standard Oil station where her father refilled his truck. My mother knew every inch of Doland. The town was hers to explore in full.

When my mother was eight, she found a family of newborn mice in the library and ran, baby rodents in hand, to show her dad outside the service station. She didn't run straight into the first-ever Black man she ever saw, but only because he spotted her coming. He was a long-haul trucker whose accent hinted that he was from somewhere south.

"Let loose of those things, little girl!" the man said in a firm voice.

My mother's father, George, laughed, acknowledged his

daughter, and then went back to talking with the trucker like they were old friends.

My mother and father admired their parents deeply. They were generous and kindhearted in all ways, not just in their racial attitudes. But just as my father couldn't fully identify the source of his parents' politics, so too was Evelyn and George's progressivism a mystery to my mother. That was especially true for my grandfather, who rarely strayed from Spink County, South Dakota. Why did Evelyn, George, Vera, and Russell believe what they believed? Was it the relatively progressive theology preached in the Methodist churches they attended? Was it a post–Great Depression populist spirit, a belief that their lot was with anybody, anywhere, who might be considered the little guy?

Or was it simply the game, soon to be repeated many times down their family line, of Whiteness contrasting itself with Whiteness, of two working-class couples from the White Upper Midwest finding meaning and pride in who they weren't—sneering, outwardly racist White southerners; genteel Bourbon aristocrats; bloodthirsty, shotgun-toting sheriffs?

Those other White people weren't mentioned explicitly in Russell Bucks's remarks to his children in Davenport, but their presence was clear.

"Boys . . . those people are wrong." Meaning, of course, *We aren't those people.*

Chapter THREE

I internalized so many lessons from our family, both those that I learned as a child and others that I'd only encountered as an adult. Lessons about what kind of people we were, what kind of neighbors we sought to be, what kind of politics we held. But those were the explicit lessons. There were other lessons that I filled in for myself, lessons about my assumed obligation to the Bucks and Gelston family line and the town that we came from. They were stories about tragedy, loss, and legacies left incomplete.

Whether by accident or collective intention, midcentury Doland, South Dakota, somehow split the difference between Evelyn Gelston's ambition and George Gelston's rootedness. Doland was not a place that had any illusions about its distinctiveness or exceptionalism compared with other tiny prairie outposts. It had a towering grain elevator and a small everything else—a school, a diner, and a firehouse. Clark and Henry and Frederick and Tulare and so many other dots on the highway had all those things as well.

And yet Doland wasn't just another prairie town. Starting in the 1930s and then continuing for the next two decades, a steady stream of its young men (always its young men, which never went unnoticed by my mother) started making big names for themselves in the world. There were the twin World War II generals Marvin and Melvin McNickle. There was the Yale theologian Julian Norris Hartt, whose students would include some of the most influential names in post-war American Christianity. And there was Hartt's high school buddy Hubert Humphrey, the "happy warrior" orator who made his name standing for civil rights against those *other* White people, the infamous southern Dixiecrats.

By the 1950s and 1960s, the old-timers in town saw the same pattern of Doland exceptionalism in the new generation. Mostly, they saw it in my mom's older brother, Ken, who was bighearted, whip-smart, and ambitious in the same way that everybody remembered Humphrey having been. He went to school in the Twin Cities, just like Humphrey, and then matriculated to Stanford Law School. In the same way that previous generations of Dolandites talked about how Hubert Humphrey was going to be president one of these days, so too was there no question as to Ken's fate. George and Evelyn's eldest was going to be a U.S. Supreme Court justice.

At least for the first few years of the 1960s, the old-timers in Doland truly believed that their town's children might change the world. Hubert Humphrey, fresh off leading the passage of the 1964 Civil Rights Act in the Senate, was now Lyndon Johnson's vice president. Ken Gelston was the editor of *Stanford Law Review*. Dan and Jane Bucks, no academic slouches themselves, were starting their own promising college careers, my father fresh from a stint at Boys Nation in Washington, D.C.

And then everything fell apart.

The first funeral was for my uncle Ken, in 1964. He died in Glacier National Park in Montana—a place where he had worked every summer since high school, a place he loved immensely, a place he taught his kid sister to love immensely as well. He was hiking with a friend and fell into Saint Mary Falls. It was a summer of horrific flooding. His was one of many lost bodies.

My grandparents never recovered from Ken's death. They had finally moved to California after George's retirement from Standard Oil, and according to my aunt Sally they didn't say a single word the entire drive up to Glacier Park. Despondent, they returned to South Dakota shortly thereafter. Evelyn found a teaching job, and George worked as a hired hand at a turkey farm.

The next two deaths came in 1966. Two freak farm accidents. February and November. Russell was crushed by the hydraulic lift on a truck. George was sucked into a tractor's power takeoff. By the time my parents got married in '67, they did so without their fathers, without the brother my mom idolized, and with their two mothers still deep in shock. It wasn't a picture-perfect wedding. It was heartbreaking, bittersweet, and utilitarian. There was a terrible thunderstorm that day, one of the worst anybody in attendance could remember.

My parents were still smart kids from Doland, now with college degrees, so they took off to do something with those degrees. They started graduate programs at Johns Hopkins University in Baltimore. As soon as the prairie kids arrived in town, the student services office gave them a map of north Baltimore with a narrow rectangle of safety carved out for where they, a nice young White couple, were supposed to live.

My mother was pregnant that year. It was a phenomenally tough pregnancy. My parents didn't have any money, so they went to a furniture store on Charles Street, searching for the cheapest possible crib. The White store proprietor guided them away from their affordable first choice, helpfully informing them that it was a piece of crap, a fire trap, and that he sold it only to, you know, *them*. My parents don't remember if he used the word or not.

In April 1968, Martin Luther King Jr. was killed in Memphis. Baltimore went up in flames, as did so many other cities. According to news reports, the furniture store on Charles Street was one of the first businesses to be torched.

Just a few weeks later, late at night on May 2, my mother was rushed to Union Memorial Hospital. The Black hospital. The poor people's hospital. The whole building was dimly lit and foreboding, both inside and out. My parents were later assured that had they gone to a different hospital, a White people's hospital, the baby likely would have survived.

It was a horrific night. My father, four floors removed from my mother, wasn't allowed to visit her until the next morning. Screams echoed all night long throughout the open maternity ward, the shrieks coming from everywhere and nowhere in particular. After the baby girl was officially pronounced dead, she was placed in a big metal bowl off to the side. My mom kept begging to hold her, to no avail.

They left Baltimore that summer, defeated, hopeless, mourning. The night of June 6, they were up late packing, listening to Robert Kennedy's victory speech after the California primary. Kennedy's campaign was one of their few remaining sources of hope. Like many young progressives of their generation, my parents were inspired by his youth, his firm stance against the Vietnam War, and his increasingly passionate statements about racial and economic justice. If Kennedy were to win, 1968 might still be something other than a tragedy.

The next morning, they woke up to the news that Kennedy too was dead. Like his brother. Like King. Like Ken, Russell, and George. Like their baby.

They returned to South Dakota. It was all too much to metabolize so quickly—our country's original sin, laid bare and impossible to ignore, violence both generalized and specific. In the middle of it all, left on the street in Baltimore, a cruel take on Hemingway's six-word story: For sale, crib-shaped totem of America's moral failings, never used.

My parents moved into a tiny apartment next to a Dairy Queen in Brookings. My dad found summer work at South Dakota State University. My mom was pregnant again, but all signs pointed to yet another painful miscarriage. There were more close calls. Hemorrhages. Emergency hospital visits.

The world around them kept falling apart. Nothing was as it should be, either thousands of miles away, as war raged in Vietnam, or immediately on their block. Brookings felt pre-apocalyptic that summer. The man who lived in the trailer closest to them kept a live tiger captive in a metal enclosure. My mother and father fell asleep to the sound of its growls.

The next death came on a particularly hot summer day. It was an anonymous death. My mother walked outside just in time to see a garbage truck run over a three-year-old boy, right in front of his older sister. They had gone out for a treat at the Dairy Queen.

On August 29, 1968, Doland's own Hubert Humphrey accepted the nomination for presidency of the United States at the old Chicago International Amphitheatre, a hulking brick fortress on Halsted Street. The venue was on the South Side, directly adjacent to the stockyards, the place where the Black urban Midwest and the rural White Midwest reencountered each other every single day, the place where Russell Bucks once took Dan and Dale to stay in Black hotels and eat in Black restaurants and offer them an unspoken lesson that they were to build a kinder world than the one they had inherited.

August 29 was not a night for a gentle farmer's tender hopes for his boys, though. That night, Martin Luther King Jr. was still dead and Baltimore was still a pile of rubble and the bombs were still falling on Vietnam and, a few miles away from the International Ampitheatre, the hippies on the street outside the Conrad Hilton Hotel took so many of the Chicago Police Department's billy clubs to so many skulls.

The hippie kids had come to Chicago to stop Humphrey's nomination. He was Lyndon Johnson's vice president, which meant that his earlier civil rights bona fides meant nothing now. The blood from the war was on his hands. They chanted "the whole world is watching" as the blows from middle-aged cops with Polish and Italian last names kept coming. The whole world was, in fact, watching. The TV stations were reporting live.

That night my father, whom I have never seen drunk and have rarely heard curse, sat in front of a crappy television set, crushing can after can of beer and screaming obscenities at his country, his political party, and even at his fellow Dolandite, a man who once left a floor debate on the Farm Bill to make sure that a wide-eyed Boys Nation delegate from Doland knew that there was a place for him in the cradle of American democracy.

His anger was spontaneous and primal and never again to be repeated for the remainder of his life. My father got it all out of his system in one night.

After that disastrous summer, my parents picked up the pieces and attempted to build something out of the rubble. They had no choice. Seven months after the Democratic National Convention, my oldest brother, Eric, was born. Safe. Sound. And after some initial breastfeeding difficulties, completely healthy. A break in the storm, and not the last.

Colin came next, then Brian, then Nate, then a gap, then me, then Anna. My mom put every ounce of herself—her drive and creativity and idealism—into us. She worked outside of the house at times and was always active in the politics of the communities where she lived. But none of what she took on was in service of a clear personal ambition. And that was a choice she made, proudly. When people asked my mother how it felt having that many boys, she'd say that she loved it because it gave her the opportunity to raise five committed feminists.

By the time I was born, in 1981, the decades of death and uncertainty were in the rearview. All of us Bucks siblings were enveloped in unconditional love and support. Ours was a cacophonous, filled-to-the-brim house where all our voices mattered and none of us had to fear loneliness. It was neither my parents' nor my siblings' fault that I heard about Ken and Hubert and Doland and assumed that there was an unfinished story that I was obligated to complete.

But that is the story that I believed, even before I knew all the tragic details of deaths and retreat. I felt guilty for it all. I was obsessed, even at a young age, with the fear that I hadn't earned the love and intentionality that enveloped me every day.

When I was six years old, I would play with my Lego bricks on the kitchen floor while my mother cooked dinner. I didn't have Lego Minifigures, so I took one brick—a big yellow rectangle with a smiley face on it that I had named Prince Smiley—who would travel from his safe, comfortable home to far-off countries filled with more interestingly shaped bricks (bridge supports, tall and slender and curving into an R, were some of my go-tos). He would inform the new, different-looking bricks that he had come to them with the most important mission in the world: he was looking for love.

Chapter FOUR

I do have a story about the first moment I truly discovered my own Whiteness, one that felt too revealing for a diversity-training circle.

I was seven. My dad was about to head back to the D.C. metro area, where he had started commuting for a new job. My brother Eric was leaving too, returning to college in Iowa. Sending my father off to work and Eric off to school earlier in the year were both among the first moments that I felt our house becoming emptier rather than fuller, and I hated it.

To help cheer me up, my parents drove up Interstate 15 to Montana City to rent Steven Spielberg's 1982 science fiction hit, *E.T. the Extra-Terrestrial*. While we'd eventually get a VCR of our own, "renting a movie" meant carting home not just the film itself but the machine on which to play it. A special occasion.

E.T. is often credited as one of the first modern blockbuster films—for an entire decade after its release, it was the highest-grossing movie in history. In the film, a boy named

Elliott, who lives in a hazy Los Angeles exurb with his divorced mom, protective older brother, and precocious younger sister, encounters a kindly, wayward alien. The two develop an intense, symbiotic relationship, one that is tested by sickness and a judgmental world of uncurious adults and paranoid institutions. They eventually overcome those challenges together, and Elliott assists the alien in returning to his home planet. I was enraptured.

As I lay in bed that night, I couldn't stop thinking about the movie. I was hyperaware of every way Elliott was like me: a White middle-class boy. We weren't identical, but that didn't matter. Elliott grew up in a suburban cul-de-sac on the edge of a giant metropolitan area. I grew up thousands of miles north on Interstate 15, close to nobody except my own family and a single neighbor. Elliott could ride his bike from street to street for what felt like miles. If I rode too far down our driveway, I'd first hit the frontage road, then the interstate, and then I'd be stuck. Elliott's parents were divorced, his mother visibly grieving. My parents were together, fully in love, fully in partnership.

I noticed, in a way that I hadn't noticed while watching so many White boys in so many prime-time sitcoms, that this boy who reminded me of myself was intended to stand in for every audience member watching him. He was supposed to be as ordinary and relatable as possible, such that his delight, his tears, and his triumph could be our own.

I watched Elliott and cried because, for half the movie, he hadn't done anything to deserve being an audience surrogate.

Other than his parents' divorce, there was nothing special about him. And yet it was him that we were watching, surrounded by the comforts of middle-class White suburbia: a fridge full of name-brand food, a room full of electronic toys, a closet packed almost to explosion with stuffed animals. I didn't have the vocabulary or perspective that night to recognize that if Elliott's story was meant to be *everybody's* story, it meant that so many other stories weren't blessed with that universality—women's stories, Black and Brown stories, poor people's stories. What I did know, though, was that White boy had gained the world's sympathy, even though he, like I, hadn't earned it.

Elliott and I had been given so many gifts—material gifts, spiritual gifts, societal gifts, gifts of love and attention. And after receiving all those gifts, after having a world built in our name, we were still just average, normal, blank slates of White all-American boy banality.

Later, when rewatching *E.T.* as an adult, I realized that the film is about Elliott's unremarkable Whiteness being punctured through contact, about a White boy being born again in the moment he meets a wise, magical being whose way of existing is literally alien to him. It's a movie about how, if a nice White boy befriends somebody noticeably different from himself, the two entities will eventually develop such a powerful sympathetic connection that they will become one, a single being split between two bodies.

At the time of filming, the White citizens of Tujunga, California—the town where *E.T.* was shot—were immersed in a bitter battle to keep their children from being bused to a school with a higher percentage of Black and Brown students. The fictional story of a White boy becoming fully alive through alien contact ironically coincided with a real-world story of a White community resisting contact with human beings of other races by any means necessary.

I didn't know all that as I lay in bed that night at the end of winter break. I didn't know about White mothers screaming at politicians who dared to send their kids to school with Black and Brown children.

What I did know now was that, like Elliott, I was *just a White boy*.

This realization meant that a world had been built for me, which filled me with both grief and an entirely self-centered sense of purpose. If I could never meet an alien, I would need to prove that I was special by some other means. I would have to live a life worthy of the legacy of multiple generations of Buckses and Gelstons—farmers and schoolteachers and fuel truck drivers who, in my imagination at least, had all successfully built a life at the intersection of ambition and kindness. I would have to live a White life that didn't waste two generations' worth of unexpected levels of thoughtfulness on issues of race. Most important, I would have to live a life worthy of Dan and Jane Bucks's intentionality, a life that didn't waste all these inputs—the benefit dinners and my mother's choice to forego her own career to raise us and the gentle but clear messages about our responsibility to the world.

PART TWO

What I Learned in School

Chapter FIVE

Two years before that viewing of *E.T.*, I began my academic career at Clancy Elementary School. I proudly toted a brand-new Peter Pan backpack onto the same yellow bus as my brother Nate, traveling ten minutes south on the frontage road to the mismatched collection of time capsule buildings that housed various K–8 classrooms. Clancy School was a revelation. I wasn't the small brother lost in a huge crowd of much larger brothers. I was a part of something. I was a Merry Mouse, a member of Ms. Smith-Patterson's class.

I loved being a Merry Mouse. I loved riding the bus with my best friends, a set of twins who weren't named Stacey and Pacey but who let me call them Stacey and Pacey. I loved learning about letters and scissors and Hawaii (there was an entire unit about Hawaii, the place least like Clancy, Montana, any Merry Mouse could imagine!). I didn't love the overly loud bell in Clancy School's old gym, but I loved that all the Merry Mice were equally scared of its brittle clanging.

I'd long watched my brothers go off and become a part of a "we"—cross-country teams and youth groups and 4-H clubs. And now, with the Merry Mice, I had my "we." I already had the sense that, as proud as I was to be a Bucks, my family was required to love me. The fact that I was a Merry Mouse, though, meant that there was a group of people who had the choice to reject me but didn't.

There was so much that I noticed but didn't process, like how the Merry Mice weren't actually all alike, that some of our parents had jobs at desks in offices in Helena, others' parents worked outside for a living, and some parents didn't work at all.

I knew that only White people lived in and around Clancy, but I didn't think that was odd or notable. Even after my parents started dutifully introducing me to a world of racial diversity, I assumed that people who weren't White just preferred to live in other places. In Montana, a state where most people were either White or Native, Clancy was White, Browning was Blackfeet, Arlee was Salish, and Crow Agency was Crow.

That last one made particular sense. Of course the Crow lived in Crow Agency. Where else would the Crow live? And, by that same logic, where else would White people live but Clancy, a town whose namesake, "Judge" William Clancey, would have been entirely forgotten to history had he not followed the gold rush to Montana. There is no definitive historical record of a William Clancey prior to his arrival in the West; he likely came from Michigan, but that may have been an entirely different man with the same name. He was almost certainly not a real judge. He was a White man searching for treasure who knew enough to print the legend and eventually drop the unnecessary *e* from his surname.

During the eight years my family lived off of that frontage road, we had only one neighbor within walking distance. Like William Clancey, he was a gold prospector, one of the last of his kind. His name was Bunchy, and he'd plow our driveway in the winter and put on a little show for us on Halloween (hiding in his house and running out in costume to surprise the only family that had any reason to knock on his door every year). So it all made sense to me. I lived in a town named for a White gold prospector because that was where the White gold prospectors lived.

————

The story of how my little town actually became White isn't exactly hidden. Clancy is in Jefferson County, Montana, which in turn is one of hundreds of American places named for America's third President.

Thomas Jefferson was many things, including a man with an extremely high opinion of his own intellect. Jefferson believed he had figured out the entire world and all of its inhabitants. He had theories about Black people, whom he believed to be less civilized than Whites and therefore less deserving of freedom. But he also held theories about poor Whites, whom Jefferson and his peers referred to as "waste people." Because they were poor and uneducated, their presence threatened to undermine Jefferson's theory of White supremacy. But because they were White, they could be saved, as long as they stayed out of view. To Jefferson, the solution was the frontier: the less worthy White people could get their own plot of land, out of sight of the grand plantations, where they could, over time, amass their own riches. The children of the "waste people," in turn, would be sent to school. If all went to plan, White poverty would be eliminated. If the project failed, at least that failure would be far from view.

Go west, President Jefferson told Lewis and Clark. *Explore the uncharted Native lands, make them America, and make it so that every anonymous White prospector can one day have his own patch of heaven named after him and every eager White schoolchild can be a Merry Mouse.*

I first learned that my family would be leaving Clancy the summer of 1988, just as I was about to start second grade. My dad worked in the Revenue Department for the State of Montana, but his boss was a Democratic governor who had reached his term limit. It was clear that the next administration wouldn't have a role for my father, which necessitated a national search for an organization looking for his specific skill set. My dad was an expert in tax code, and particularly excelled in finding and closing loopholes that were frequently exploited by massive corporations. He eventually found a nonprofit based in Washington, D.C., but the organization needed him to start sooner than was feasible for a Montana household full of school-aged children, chickens, and ducks. That's why he had to return to D.C. that Christmas when I watched *E.T.* He was our family's advance party for our big move. For a while, I kept the news to myself. I didn't fully believe it was happening.

I finally told my class about the move in January 1989. For weeks, recess was a constant barrage of questions: Would I meet the president? Would I live in the White House. Would I write back if my classmates wrote to me?

My family moved in March. My class was in the middle of reading *The Phantom Tollbooth* together. That too is the story of a White boy, Milo, whose life is not merely ordinary but boring. Unlike Elliott, Milo must leave his home behind to find salvation. He travels to a world full of talking dogs and anthropomorphic letters and numbers. There are bickering monarchs and failed governments and demons around every corner. But because Milo is a curious, bookish hero with a big heart, he eventually saves that world before returning home. Once again, message received.

On my last day, the other second-graders in Ms. Carter's class gifted me my own copy so that I could read along with them as my family drove to Maryland. They all signed it, Stacey and Pacey and the rest of my friends. They filled the acknowledgments page with bubble letters and pillowy cursive loops. The hope inherent in that gift was that we would always be connected. I cradled the book with pride as we started our drive east, fully intending to keep that promise.

Chapter SIX

After struggling to find an affordable house large enough for our family close to Washington, D.C., we finally settled in Columbia, Maryland. In Columbia, I caught the bus behind my cul-de-sac to Thunder Hill Elementary School. I was told that my street, Broken Lute Way, was named for a line in an Oliver Wendell Holmes poem called "The Voiceless." As should be expected from that title, it's a fairly depressing composition: the lyres are all busted, there is death everywhere, and those who are still living have earned "the cross without the crown of glory."

All the streets in our subdevelopment had names borrowed from Holmes's poems. That was novel. Back in Clancy, my official address didn't exist on any map; we were instead saddled with the mail carrier's code: Star Route, Box 1. But in Columbia, it was works of dour Anglo-Saxon art all the way down. That's how I first learned that I now lived in a planned community, where everything was in its right place, where there wasn't a publicly elected city government but every neighborhood had a very nice swimming pool.

Cities like Columbia—usually unincorporated and located on the edges of large, coastal metropolitan areas—were products of a particular midcentury American optimism. The latter half of the twentieth century inspired more than one successful real estate developer to create American free market utopias where all the world's social ills might disappear, and Columbia was one of the most prominent and long-lived of those experiments.

The city that would be our Maryland home was birthed in a series of mid-sixties boardrooms. It was the product of both James Rouse's vision and the collective effort of a whole graduate school's worth of well-credentialed sociologists, urban planners, educational researchers, economists, and real estate developers.

Born on Maryland's Eastern Shore and coming into prominence after World War II, Rouse was an early proponent of the 1950s-era Baltimore Plan, which aimed to redevelop the industrial city's sprawling slums. He then turned his attention to commerce—first to suburban shopping malls and later to the construction of downtown festival marketplaces (like Boston's Faneuil Hall and Baltimore's Harborplace) that served as harbingers for urban gentrification. Each success convinced him that racism and economic stratification weren't inevitable outgrowths of American history, but the results of poor planning.

The town he envisioned as "The Next America" was to

be an unincorporated but micromanaged oasis that would prove that racial and economic integration was both possible and good for business. There was perhaps no better example of these parallel impulses rubbing against each other than the boxy, utilitarian interfaith centers where I spent my peak squirmy church-pew years. By concentrating religious institutions in interfaith centers rather than allowing for freestanding places of worship, Rouse freed up more land that could be developed and sold for a profit rather than held by nonprofit, nonrevenue-generating faith communities.

In Columbia, Muslims, Jews, and Christians worshipped at our allotted hours and then handed the space off to the next group of adherents. As we did so, we both tested Rouse's ideal that such centers would promote religious intermixing and made the Rouse Company more money.

But of all the choices Rouse made, none was more utopian than his dream of true integration. It was with this dream in mind that the Rouse Company, through its benevolently dictatorial Columbia Association, decreed that all our villages would have a mix of housing types and price points. It was why it further decreed a set of mechanisms to ensure that if any single village became too White, too Black, too Latino, or too Asian, then home sales would stall until a proper integrative balance was restored.

By the time my family moved there in 1989, Columbia had grown to more than one hundred thousand residents in nine distinct villages. My village, Dorsey's Search, was one of the newest developments. Thunder Hill Elementary was in

Oakland Mills—an older village whose tree cover was more mature and whose streets were named for images in Andrew Wyeth paintings.

At Thunder Hill, I learned that diversity was a good thing. My classmates were Black, White, and Asian. Back in Montana, there was one Black man into whom I ran headfirst. At initial glance, Columbia looked like a true melting pot. Though years later I heard Columbia described as an overwhelmingly White place, it was by far the least White place I had lived.

Back in Clancy, there was only Christmas. Here in Maryland, there was Ramadan and Hanukkah and so many other holidays. Some of the people who celebrated the different holidays weren't White, but some were. My Jewish classmates were mostly White like me, I learned, but it was complicated. They had a shared story of tragedy—perhaps past tense, perhaps present tense—that was foreign to me. But Thunder Hill treated them like the rest of its White kids, which is to say that it didn't treat them like it treated its Black kids.

I learned that of all the ways to be special, the most important one of all was to be smart. Being gifted and talented was the floor. The real aim was to be accepted into accelerated programs at the Center for Talented Youth at Johns Hopkins. There were patterns as to who was considered a sufficiently "talented youth" to justify being plucked from Thunder Hill to attend those specialized programs. For while our school was the kind of space that we were supposed to be proud to attend together—our little rainbow coalition of various racial, religious, and class groups—it was also a space that classified us, that sought to make sense of which ones of us were special enough to deserve more opportunities.

My family presented a problem for the very idea of Columbia, because Columbia wasn't truly interested in integration—it cared about sorting. Columbia wanted every group present and accounted for, but each in its proper place. Some Columbians, it was assumed, *chose* to live here, which is to say that they could have lived in a Whiter and less intentional place. Other Columbians were *lucky* to live here, blessed with the benevolence of their high-minded neighbors.

The Bucks family was a threat to this logic because we weren't easily sorted. On the one hand, we passed that community's core existential tests: we were White and my parents had college degrees; my father worked for a nonprofit in D.C.; we had even traded in our old Vanagon for a new Dodge Caravan. There were no jalopies in our driveway.

On the other hand, we were from the kind of place where poor, backward people lived. Having spent a significant part of our educational careers being taught in presumably backwoods, redneck schools, my siblings and I were suspect.

Though my family fulfilled part of the Jeffersonian ideal by moving out west, we failed at the second part: to stay hidden. Each of the schools that my siblings and I matriculated to in Maryland sought to solve our inscrutability with pseudo-objective logic. My mother was summoned to meetings with all our principals. One by one, they explained that while we were well-behaved and understood the course material, we weren't quite Howard County Public Schools material. My brother Colin, who arrived in Columbia as a senior, wasn't allowed to graduate with his new class because the assumption was that four years of high school in Montana wasn't at the same level as four years in a Howard County high school. He had to fly back to Jefferson High School to receive his diploma at his old school. As for me, I was declared a struggling reader and placed in various support classes—not because of my actual reading ability, but because of apparent poor performance on an alphabetization exercise.

Even at the time, I noticed that those groups were Blacker and that the pulled-out gifted and talented students were all White and Asian. Another message received. Because I was deemed to be White trash, I was, like the Black kids, a problem that the system needed to solve, an object of sympathy and scrutiny.

By the fall of third grade, I stopped sleeping through the night. Every night, I thrashed about my bed and sweated through my clothes before finally calling it quits and begging my parents to join them in their bed. The stomachaches started around the same time. They were worse during school hours. From the moment the bus pulled up to Thunder Hill to the moment it dropped me off at Broken Lute Way, it felt like a hundred tiny knives were jabbing me in the abdomen.

My parents took me to doctors all over the Baltimore-Washington metro area to figure out what was wrong with me. None of them could explain my predicament. In the spring of 1990, one of those doctors finally diagnosed me with Crohn's disease, a chronic inflammation of the GI tract. None of the other specialists had a better theory, so we went with it. The treatment for Crohn's came with side effects (the medication could cause nausea, vomiting, headaches, and constant fatigue), though, and that gave my mother pause. Right before pulling the trigger on my first dose, she took me to Johns Hopkins for one final opinion.

We don't remember the name of the doctor at Johns Hopkins. He looked and sounded like all the other White male specialists whose offices I had been paraded through. He was tall, but all those doctors seemed tall. What made him stand out was that he didn't quickly launch into a lecture about his vast medical knowledge. Instead, he asked my mother and me how school was going. It didn't take very long of listening to our answers to determine that I did not, in fact, have Crohn's disease; I was homesick.

My parents took it from there. They gave me anxiety-relief exercises and bribed me with baseball cards when I successfully slept through the night. After a year, all the benefits of Whiteness (and especially the way in which American educators often respond to a White mother advocating for her White children) kicked in as well—neither I nor any of my siblings would ever be fully discarded by the American school system.

I learned my lesson, though. From that point on, I would make sure I was never again mistaken for a redneck. I would always be the smartest person in the room.

Chapter SEVEN

The primary lesson of Dunloggin Middle School, where I matriculated after fifth grade at Thunder Hill, was that middle school is awful. I learned what it felt like to get shoved into the creek behind the school and to be on the receiving end of strong right hooks to the face. It wasn't the physical pain that stuck with me; it was looking up and seeing faces gathered around—some laughing, others sympathetic; all of them separate from me, reminding me I was alone.

I didn't fully understand why I was targeted for bullying. I mean, I was awkward: gangly, freckle-faced, and prone to spastic arm movements. But physically awkward kids are a dime a dozen in middle schools. It didn't make sense.

At Thunder Hill, I could tell a story as to why teachers thought I was a dumb hick. By middle school, I thought I blended in—I had clawed my way up to the honors classes, dressed in a baggy Stüssy shirt and a pair of khaki board shorts, and cheered for the Baltimore Orioles. I tried to make myself a mirror image of my bullies, all of whom were White boys like me. But it wasn't enough.

I was self-centered, but I don't mean that in the sense of only focusing on my own advancement. I mean that I was literally unaware of anybody but me. I was a wounded White boy who only saw my own situational marginality. Settled into my identity as a victim, I was less curious about the space I took up or what was going on for anybody around me.

I couldn't tell you what Dunloggin was like for the Black kids, few of whom were in my honors classes. Nor could I tell you what it was like for its Asian kids, a category I mentally sorted into two groups: kids who had grown up in the States, who were in my honors classes, and whose houses in which I'd sometimes hang out and play Sega, and the kids whom the more established Asian American kids called FOBs (Fresh Off the Boat), who were corralled away in English as a second language classes. I definitely couldn't tell you what Dunloggin was like for Latino or Middle Eastern kids, each of whom numbered in the single digits. I couldn't even really tell you what it was like for its girls (of any race).

At least for the first year or so of middle school, this self-narrative was uncomplicated. There was a clear breaking point, though, midway through seventh grade. There was life before the bus ride and life after the bus ride.

This was in the era when multiple authority figures encouraged me to defend myself. My father even signed me up for karate lessons. I couldn't stand those lessons. I could never imagine myself actually using any of the techniques I learned in class. At least some of that reticence had to do with my pacifism, but that wasn't all of it. I couldn't imagine being able to summon a sufficient enough physical force to deter the confident White boys who bullied me.

It is meaningful, then, which bully I knew, even subconsciously, that I could hurt.

I don't remember his name nor what he said, only that it was cruel and spoken in a thick accent. I most certainly never learned which East Asian country his family had recently arrived from. On the days when I rode the bus, he was on it, so there had been plenty of opportunities to get to know him, but I never took them. He said something mean. Again, I can't even remember what. But this time, unlike with all the White bullies, I lashed back. I stood up, turned around, and yelled, "I guess they didn't teach you manners in your ESL classes!"

I remember his punch much more than the others. He had a strong jab. He was furious, but I could also see the hint of tears welling up in his eyes. I saw that he wanted to keep punching me. If the bus driver hadn't lurched to a halt and threatened to come back there, I swear he'd still be punching me.

I remember running home to my mother, receiving perfect, pure, unconditional sympathy for a few minutes before telling her the whole story, before admitting to her that the other boy didn't just punch me for no reason, that I had said something—something that I knew was cruel. And though I hadn't chosen those words with the explicit hope of saying something racist, I had wanted them to sting.

I remember Jane Bucks's face dropping. I remember

watching her process in real time how to balance sympathy and accountability, how to make it clear that she was sorry I had gotten punched with incredulity about what I had done.

There are a million details I don't remember about that day, but I do remember the absolute crashing wave of shame that washed over me. It was the first moment I considered the other boy. I imagined a conversation he was having with his mother, which is to say that I was imagining mostly what his mother must be thinking of the central casting White American boy who was racist to her son. I wasn't actually considering him or his mother, though. I was concerned about what they must be thinking about me.

Chapter EIGHT

My family moved back to Montana in the fall of 1995. We did so because my grandma Evelyn, who had relocated there herself a decade previously, was now going blind. Going back to Montana meant that she could move in with us. But that wasn't the only reason. We returned because my mom had made a promise that whenever life took us away from Montana—away from a very specific set of memories and a very specific burial ground in East Glacier Park—that we would find our way back again. My dad convinced the tax nonprofit to let him work remotely, and the Maryland experiment was over. We were back home.

We moved to Missoula, a leafy college town surrounded on all sides by lush green mountains and bisected by the mighty Clark Fork River. Historically, Missoula was a bloody battleground. At various points the Salish, Kootenai, Flathead, Pend d'Oreille, Blackfeet, and Shoshone Nations wrestled for control of its fertile, cocooned flatlands. When you enter Missoula Valley from the west, you do so through a narrow canyon.

Hundreds of years ago, the Salish arrived on that route, only to be caught in a vicious Blackfeet ambush. The Salish lost the day, but their name for the canyon, Hellgate, stuck.

The Salish, Pend d'Oreille, and Kootenai all had some presence in the valley in 1855, when they were fully pushed out by the U.S. Calvary and one of the many bad-faith treaties by which the West was won. From that point forward, Missoula was officially White and open for business. At varying points in its history, Missoula was a railroad town, a lumber town, a mill town, an army town, a hub town for area farmers, ranchers, and roughnecks, and, thanks to the University of Montana, which opened in 1893, a college town.

By the 1960s and 1970s, though, when postwar White prosperity and federal support for higher education opened the door to college for millions of baby boomer young people like my parents, certain college towns—particularly college towns in idyllic western locales—adopted a new identity. Cities like Missoula became places where the more counterculture-inclined members of this newly educated, newly emboldened generation retreated from the world.

When I arrived in Missoula in 1995, it was still possible to see Missoula's varied pasts layered on top of one another like the geologic striations on the mountains that rose above it. It was still home to the railroad-yard drifters, the paper mill graveyard shift heshers, the acid-fried sixties dropouts, the elk-hunting RV dealership owners, the underemployed freelance writers, the Patagonia-clad tech millionaires, and the full-time short-order cooks/part-time punk rock bassists.

It was also still Salish and Kootenai and Pend d'Oreille and Blackfeet; even if most of Missoula's Natives had been cast out elsewhere, the towns Indigenous population still hovered somewhere between one and two thousand, with a number of tribes represented. So many other ethnic groups who played a key role in Missoula's history had been erased more definitively: the Black Buffalo Soldiers who were once stationed at Fort Missoula; the Chinese who built the railroads but whose mass graves in the Rattlesnake Valley were, until very recently, never given the dignity of commemoration or delineation; the migrant farmers from all over the world who helped Missoula earn its proud "Garden City" moniker.

We moved to a house just off the University of Montana's campus, directly in the shadow of Mount Sentinel, one of the two mountains that flank Hellgate Canyon. Our home was modest and faded blue but would soon become larger and bright white when we built an addition for my grandma. It was a few blocks from the university's central Oval, a few blocks from Freddy's Feed and Read bookstore and coffeehouse, and just one block from Bonner Park, with its old concrete bandshell and lovingly worn splash pad. A few blocks farther, up Higgins Avenue, brought Rockin' Rudy's, the record store where I spent much of my free time, and the bars and head shops of downtown: the Joint Effort, where the burnouts bought new pipes; Jay's Upstairs, where the punks played in front of an old-timey western bar corral; AmVets, a veterans bar by day, gay dance club by night.

Back then, my family could afford a house in the University

District. It was a neighborhood where doctors, lawyers, and professors lived in stately Victorians, but it was also home to cheaper houses and ramshackle rentals.

My parents enrolled me at a Catholic school, Loyola Sacred Heart—the first and last time they sent any of their six kids to a private school. They did it because it had a smaller student body than the public Hellgate High, and that meant fewer tough guys swinging at me. My parents proposed that I try out Loyola and, if I liked it after my freshman year, I'd find a job to pay for tuition. I was still shaken by Dunloggin, so I didn't put up a fight. School fees were cheap, as far as private schools went—affordable enough that by junior and senior year I was paying over 80 percent of my tuition costs from after-school hourly restaurant wages.

I ended up liking that deal.

I really liked the restaurant dish pits and prep kitchens that the deal ensured would play a large part in my high school experience. I started at Finnegan's, a twenty-four-hour diner straddling Rattlesnake Creek, before jumping to a brightly painted take-out taqueria, El Topo Azul.

I had a few teachers in those kitchens: Randy was a quiet guy with a couple of kids who went to church and liked to hunt. He didn't talk much but could handle the worst breakfast rush without breaking a sweat.

Tim was wiry, excitable, prone to "Hell yeahs!" and exaggerated countertop pounds when a song he loved came on the radio. He was in a few bands himself. He knew they'd never make it big, but he just loved to play, man.

Joe might have been on meth, but he was definitely a drunk. He'd polish off bottles of Gato Negro in the walk-in during the dinner rush. Joe was uncommonly kind to me, patient with my clumsy knife skills and adolescent stammering. He told me stories after work—about his career as a chef, about the legendary Seattle punk bands he'd been buddies with, about traveling the world. Joe was a liar. Everybody in the Missoula restaurant scene knew that Joe was a liar. But I loved that he wanted to lie to me.

They were good teachers, these guys. They taught me how to cook, talk to girls, and make better mixtapes. I'd come in and complain about this or that dreg of high school drama and they'd remind me that it didn't matter.

I didn't want their lives, though. Due to my time in Maryland, I now thought of myself as someone who would receive awards and accolades at several higher education institutions and settle down into a well-compensated white-collar job where I didn't work with my hands. I already had one foot out the door.

I also liked Loyola Sacred Heart well enough, though it's hard to say if I learned much about Catholicism. One day, in Mass, I instinctively followed the line of students going up to the altar to receive the Eucharist. As a Methodist, I wasn't supposed to receive the host in a Catholic church, but the fear of being rejected in a new space took over. I shuffled my way into line and then panicked. I knew something was wrong. What if the priest knew I wasn't Catholic? Not wanting to go to hell, but also not wanting to draw attention to myself,

I took the sacrament anyway and then—in a manner that I thought was surreptitious but probably wasn't at all—slid the body of Christ into my pocket, where it was eventually transformed into a heretical pile of crumbs.

I stuck around Loyola after my first year, partially because I liked most of the kids and partially because I really didn't want to switch schools again. Plus, Loyola had a speech and debate team that had won fifteen straight state championships, a Montana record for any activity. In that sense, it was the perfect landing spot for a kid raised on tales of the legendary debaters of Doland, South Dakota. My debate partner and I even won the state policy debate title as sophomores. And to think that the Howard County school system thought I was remedial. *How do you like me now, Johns Hopkins Center for Talented Youth?*

Because I was back in Montana, both my high school and those restaurant kitchens were mostly White, though not totally White. There were a few Salish kids, which meant there were also some White guys who would call them "prairie n******" or talk about how they should go back to the reservation with the other drunk Indians. Those same White guys—guys with pickup trucks and chew bottles who knew how to hunt and knew how to handle their liquor around a bonfire—would treat a lot of kids like crap: girls, queer kids, kids they suspected of being queer. Some of the cruelest guys would eventually come out of the closet themselves. Even more of them would eventually grow up to be kinder, wiser, and full of regrets. At the time, all of them were figuring it out.

But that's not the lesson I took away back then. Those guys were jerks, I decided, which was how I figured that by crafting an identity distinct enough from their whole deal, I got to be a good guy.

What I discovered in Missoula—where the hippies and the heshers shared space but judged each other mightily—was that I could play the game as well as any other White person. So that's what I did: Other guys hunted; I became a vegetarian. They drank; I opted for sobriety. They wore Nikes; I did a presentation in tenth-grade social studies on how Phil Knight was a criminal because his company owned sweatshops in Indonesia. They referred to girls, queer, and Salish kids with words I'd never use.

I thrived at Loyola. I knew my place. I knew my foils. I didn't have many doubts about the path I had put myself on—I was a leftist iconoclast, but I was also high achieving. I had multiple rich lives outside of school.

I felt certain enough of myself that the moments when I felt unsteady felt like jolts from a perma-state of relative comfort. The most jarring of those jolts came on a single day, April 20, 1999.

While I tend to start my life story in Clancy, that isn't technically accurate. Clancy is the first place I *remember* growing up, but I was born in Littleton, Colorado, where my family lived for a brief pit stop between two different Montana residencies. I don't have any memories of Littleton, which is why, when I was in Clancy, I pictured suburban Whiteness as something distant and unknowable. I wasn't ashamed of that blip in my biography, but until that day in April, few people had any frame of reference for the town. It was just one speck in the larger mass of Colorado Front Range sprawl.

On April 20, 1999, though, the entire world knew about Littleton, Colorado, because two White kids exactly my age, Dylan Klebold and Eric Harris, walked into Columbine High School with a full arsenal of weapons and killed thirteen of their classmates.

The massacre took place around 11:00 a.m. mountain time. As word spread around the school, the regular business of the academic day stopped with a lurch. I can't remember how we herded into the chemistry room to debrief, but I was grateful that I didn't have to pretend I wasn't shaken.

Mr. Mattson, the amiable, slightly hippieish chemistry teacher, was tasked with facilitating our ad hoc discussion, likely because his room was one of the few in the school large enough to squeeze in as much of the senior class as possible. Mr. Mattson wheeled a TV cart in front of the makeshift lecture hall he had constructed on one side of his classroom. We all watched the news for a bit, and then he turned it off and said something to the effect of, "So, any thoughts?"

I didn't want to share what I was actually thinking. I didn't want to admit that I felt implicated somehow in all this, bound up in it. I had no memories of Littleton, but I really had been an infant there, which meant that my parents and brothers once walked me up and down suburban sidewalks, carting me to church and the grocery store.

Surely, at one point or another, my path crossed with other

little White infants. And if that was true, that meant I was part of a web. I was connected to the kids who ran for their lives and the kids who lay dead in the cafeteria. Most unnervingly, I was connected to a couple of White boys in trench coats with military-grade firearms. They were now scared White teens and guilty White teens and infamous White teens and dead White teens, but at one point they and I were just babies being taken around the same nondescript White suburb by our moms and dads.

I didn't know how to metabolize that particular story of interconnectedness; I only knew that it scared me. It didn't feel like whatever version of connectivity I once had with the Merry Mice. I had been frightened—ever since Dunloggin— that my race and gender, if exacerbated by self-centeredness, might make me a monster. Now I had the proof. There were two White boys—White boys I assumed were bullied just like I had been—who were now monsters. They were more monstrous than me, sure, but the fact that there was any parallel at all spooked me. I shifted uncomfortably in my seat.

I didn't share any of those thoughts, of course. Instead, I sparred with the other kids.

When the discussion started in earnest, Paul, a basketball player who liked to hunt and party and wasn't above a few racial slurs here and there, called Klebold and Harris a bunch of goth losers. I couldn't abide by that argument, of course. I shouted something back about how Klebold and Harris must have been bullied, and how, if so, that while they were guilty, their bullies should take a look in the mirror as well.

Another voice answered back—I think it belonged to Seth, another letter jacket wearer—"Come on, lots of people get bullied, but you don't see them shooting up schools." That was a good point, but I didn't want to grant it, so I changed the subject. I said something about guns. I was lost in the debate now. The point wasn't winning the argument. The point was that I had somebody to argue against. No longer uncomfortable, I sat up a little taller in my seat.

Chapter NINE

F our years following my high school graduation, I found myself a thousand miles from home, in possession of a freshly minted Earlham College Peace and Global Studies degree and a provisional alternative certification from the New Mexico Department of Education. If Clancy, Thunder Hill, Dunloggin, and Loyola all taught me lessons about what kind of White person I was supposed to be, now was the time to officially perform those lessons. By the power vested in me by the Gallup-McKinley County School District, I was now a fifth-grade teacher at Crownpoint Elementary School, fully clothed in both leftist political righteousness and my father's and older brothers' hand-me-down khakis.

Crownpoint is in the northwest corner of New Mexico but the southeast corner of the Navajo Nation, a sprawling landmass larger than West Virginia. For decades, White people came to Crownpoint, armed with either lofty promises or violent threats. Some stayed, but most took what they needed and left.

White people invaded New Mexico in the 1500s. First came the Spanish conquistadores and then, in the 1800s, the U.S. Army. America fought a war with Mexico and won, then turned its eyes to the dozens of tribes living on the land that the cocky young country now claimed for itself. The post-colonization Diné story is as devastating as most tribes' stories. There were broken treaties. There was forced internment and death marches. There was the establishment of reservations and the attendant flood of White saviors: government agents looking for a paycheck, boarding school teachers who believed in killing the Indian to save the child, missionaries looking to bring the Diné to Christ.

There's no right way to live under colonialism. Some of the Diné resisted missionary Christianity in favor of either traditional Navajo spirituality or the more modern, pan-tribal Native American Church. Others ran toward it, working for the government, founding churches, speaking in tongues. Many Navajo warriors fought the U.S. government for as long as they could and then, when that was no longer an option, chose the only warrior path available that wouldn't get them locked up: fighting *for* the U.S. Army. Today, the Navajo Nation has some of the highest rates of miliary service in the country. The most revered heroes in contemporary Dinétah are the code talkers, the Navajo men who, in World War II, used the Diné language as the basis for the only code the Nazis could never break.

The town of Crownpoint doesn't have any deep historical significance to the Diné. The modern Navajo Nation is served by two governments: the tribal one out of Window Rock, Arizona, and the American one mediated by the Bureau of Indian Affairs. Two governments means two sets of government agencies—health departments and housing authorities and welfare bureaus and the like. Crownpoint exists because it happened to be as good a place as any to concentrate those services for the Eastern Navajo Agency.

When I lived there, Crownpoint had a gas station and a grocery store and, occasionally, a cardboard box in the middle of one of its intersections, informing its residents that Victoria was making pizzas out of her house and if you called her, she'd send one of her middle school kids out in their truck to deliver it to you.

Crownpoint is gorgeous, framed by the majestic Tee Pee Mesa on its southern edge. It's also poisoned. The town is surrounded by hundreds of now abandoned uranium mines that the U.S. government established during the heyday of the nearby Los Alamos Manhattan Project. At the time I lived there, cancer rates in Crownpoint were twice the national average.

The irony of the Indigenous Southwest is that the scientists who poisoned half the state and built a world-destroying bomb didn't actually defeat the Nazis. The people they poisoned did. Their language did—the language they carried with them all the way from Alaska, that sustained them through colonization, and that they then took to Europe to save the country that had conquered them.

I came to Crownpoint because I was a recent White college graduate trying to square a few disparate circles. I had an undergraduate degree in peace and a bookshelf full of Frantz Fanon's thoughts on colonization, Karl Marx's thoughts on capitalism, and Judith Butler's thoughts on gender. I was ready to take a sledgehammer to all the ills of the world, including those that I was afraid to find in myself, but I also needed a job that would pay off my student loans.

I also didn't just want the world to be changed; I wanted it to be very apparent that *I* was the one changing it. So I needed a certain level of prestige, but also desired more rolling-up-my-sleeves credibility than a graduate school could offer. I didn't want to sell out, but I wanted to be recognized for *doing a good thing*.

I didn't necessarily *know* anybody who had found a job that satisfied all these requirements. My parents and professors' jobs came close, but they lived more anonymous, less publicly acclaimed lives than I hoped for myself.

At various points during my senior year, I told my friends that my dream was to go organize with the Landless Workers Movement in Brazil or devote myself full-time to antiglobalization protests while living in an anarchist squat in London or Eugene, Oregon. Truth be told, I never seriously considered either option. They seemed too hard—I didn't trust myself to learn Portuguese or dumpster dive for my groceries with a bunch of unwashed anarchists and their dogs. But more so, those options felt likely to result in rejection. I was scared that the crust punks of London or the *trabalhadores* outside Belo Horizonte wouldn't like me.

Instead, I applied to Teach For America, a program that my brother Colin joined back when I was a middle schooler. TFA had been around for a decade by the time I joined. Its founder, Wendy Kopp, first conceived the idea as her Princeton undergraduate thesis in the late 1980s. Kopp's goal was to inspire a critical mass of ambitious, driven, social justice–inclined young people to make attacking the ills of America's inequitable public schools their life's work. In practice, that meant recruiting recent college graduates, offering alternative means of training and certification, and asking them to teach for at least two years in high-poverty rural or urban public schools. When I signed up in 2003, about ten thousand alumni had gone through the program, a number that would eventually grow to more than sixty thousand in subsequent years.

TFA's critics cite the organization's low retention rate in placement schools (meaning how many TFA teachers stay in their original classrooms after their required commitment) as proof that it is a neocolonial parachute-y program exacerbating the problems it sought to solve. According to those critics, Black and Brown students deserve better than some ambitious striver who may be in the classroom only to bolster their law school application.

For me, TFA offered a social justice–inclined meritocrat's dream pitch: Are you a high-achieving young person (absolutely!) who craves the cachet of selective programs (keep talking...) who also has a bleeding heart (hell yeah!)

and needs to pay off student loans (yes! urgently!)? If so, come teach in a high-poverty urban or rural school filled with Black, Brown, or Native kids. But do it with us, TFA, which means that you won't have to go through a lengthy traditional certification model, but will instead get to pass through the gates of an elite-college-style screening process and then be expected to work eighty- to ninety-hour weeks to make up for your inexperience with pure drive and pluck.

I still had my doubts, though. The TFA critiques cut to the core of my identity. I didn't want to be a missionary or colonizer. I wanted to do good work in the world, but I also wanted all the right people—progressives, radicals, Black and Brown activists—to agree that the work I had chosen was above reproach. So I was torn.

And then a week or so before Thanksgiving of my senior year, my friend Kamal, a principled and charismatic South Asian activist who had led our campus's anti-sweatshop protests before joining TFA in Atlanta, returned to campus. I peppered him with critical questions about TFA, all with the unspoken expectation that he would absolve me of my choice to apply.

Kamal told me something to the effect of: "Listen, Garrett, all your critiques—the White saviorism, the colonialism, the leaving too soon, the being bad for your kids—those are only true if you end up sucking. So, if you're scared of sucking, go off to grad school, which will be its own version of selling out, since most professors aren't really making the revolution or changing the world, they're just in ivory towers talking about it. So, if you ask me, you should join TFA and just work super hard to make sure you're not the person that you're afraid of being."

I didn't have a counterargument, so I applied. The following June, I was living in a brutalist high-rise at the University of Houston and teaching summer school at TFA's training institute.

It was one of those frenzied, exhausting, charmed summers where each day felt sixty hours long. Everything about the experience was overstuffed. I would walk out of my little portable classroom after a good day—perhaps when my students were able to work in their groups without bickering, or when they properly identified the difference between an adverb and a verb, or even when they just laughed at my jokes—and I'd pump my fist and high-five my teaching buddies as if I had just won the Super Bowl. But then after a bad day—like when my lesson on long division left my kids so frustrated they threw their pencils down on their desks, or when I tripped and dropped all the math manipulatives on the floor, or when one of my fourth-graders recoiled and yelled, *"Daaaaaamn, why your breath stink so bad?"* when I knelt down to answer a question—I'd run to the nearest faculty restroom and wheeze ugly tears.

The heat and humidity of Houston added to the overstuffedness of it all. The Gulf Coast climate felt like I was subjected to one hidden-camera-show prank after another. I sweated through my button-downs within minutes of walking outside. I dodged monsoons and trudged through flash-flooded streets. I moved as if encased in foam.

I didn't complain about the long hours or the weather or my students, though. I was surrounded by friends and buoyed by a young teacher's sense of purpose. More than all that, though, I was in love.

I had known Kjersti all four years at Earlham. We bonded over being the only kids from our respective states—Idaho and Montana—in the class of 2003. Every time we talked, I walked away grinning ear to ear, an effect she seemingly had on everybody. For most of our time on campus, though, I knew *of* her more than I knew her.

She was the much-beloved soccer captain, the polyglot who spoke English, Swedish, and French fluently, and the recipient of multiple impressive-sounding biochemistry honors. She was also the much-coveted housemate who made a Funfetti cake with rainbow icing for all her friends' birthdays, no matter the demands of her workload; the quietly charismatic campus legend who was equally at home with the hippies and the jocks and the most introverted scientists alike.

It was only in our final semester that our social networks collapsed into each other, but it didn't take long after that for her to become the most important person in my life.

We hadn't started dating until the last few months of senior year. We had spent more and more time with each other for weeks, until everything finally came together over a late

Friday night in February. Kjersti convinced me to join her and a crowd of friends for Long Island iced teas at a mall-adjacent Chili's. We went to her place afterward, silently cursing her housemates for not taking the cue and leaving us alone. When it was just us, we kissed in her cluttered communal kitchen. A perfect ending for a romantic comedy if romantic comedies were set in chain-restaurant-choked midwestern college towns.

We started dating but already knew that we were headed in different directions—me to New Mexico, Kjersti to teach English in Guadeloupe. Breaking up was the pragmatic choice, so that's what we did. The problem was that we were clearly in love. While she was supposed to be focusing on her summer research back on campus, and I was supposed to be learning how to be a teacher, we were both hopelessly distracted by thoughts of the other. The phone calls grew longer and more frequent. A couple of weeks into my training, Kjersti scrounged enough money together for a plane ticket to Houston, and by the time I dropped her off at Hobby Airport at the conclusion of that weekend together, we were all but official.

The summer flew by. My students learned most of what I tried to teach them. I didn't get nearly enough sleep, and I made terrible choices about everything I was putting into my body, but I did invent at least three different math-themed raps that my class seemed to enjoy. There were even hand motions. And props. I got a lot of compliments, especially from other TFA trainees ("I wish I had your energy!"), but at the end of the summer, the only note I remembered was one from my primary coach:

"Garrett, you're not actually supposed to be the star of your classroom—your kids are."

———

Training ended in August, at which point I headed back to Missoula to hurriedly shovel piles of hand-me-down teacher clothes, Built to Spill CDs, and bell hooks books into a used white Toyota Corolla for the drive to Crownpoint. My dad took off work to travel down with me, which meant that for the entire drive I was flooded with sense memories of past road trips we had made together. That was one more deeply sweet and intentional Dan and Jane Bucks move, recognizing that all six of us kids grew up on top of one another and so opportunities to tag along with my dad on work trips to various state capitals were precious. One of the single best memories of my middle school years was of my father and I drinking vending-machine pop and watching cable TV in a motel in Harrisburg, Pennsylvania.

We spent most of that drive on Interstate 15, the same road I once imagined would take me from Clancy to Los Angeles, toward a life where, like Elliott in *E.T.*, I would have an otherworldly encounter and I would no longer be just another unworthy White boy. This wasn't the triumphant exodus I had once imagined. What awaited me at the end of this trip wasn't an idyllic, sepia-toned California but a reservation town, a very real job, and a very real chance of failure. I was setting off to do something that many White people had already done before, often with disastrous results. I hadn't even begun teaching in Crownpoint, and I had already heard the stories of the old Bureau of Indian Affairs boarding schools, where some of my students' grandparents had their long braids cut off and their mouths washed out with soap when they were caught speaking Navajo.

As the evergreen forests of Montana gave way to the high desert of Idaho, the monied Latter-day sprawl of Salt Lake City, and, finally, the perennially sunset-hued canyons of southern Utah, I grew even more grateful that my dad was making the drive with me. We could talk about politics and baseball and rehash old family stories, and I wouldn't be alone with my thoughts. Before this drive, I worried about how I would avoid acting like a White savior. That was the fear I knew I was supposed to have, but that wasn't really what gnawed at me. My angst was much more basic than that. I feared being a complete disaster of a teacher, that my students would remember fifth grade as the worst year in their academic careers.

After two and a half days on the road, we finally made it to Crownpoint. I tracked down the school janitor to get the keys to my new home, one of roughly twenty identical Works Progress Administration fallout bunkers that the school district had repurposed as housing for its non-Native teachers. We spent a couple of days scrounging furniture from flea markets and Walmart before my father had to return home. I dropped him off at the Albuquerque International Sunport, turned back toward my dusty little teacherage, and that was that. For the first few weeks, my home phone didn't work. I walked down to the gas station and called Kjersti from a pay phone. I told her I was afraid that I would be a terrible teacher.

"Well, you probably are," she told me, before adding, "So what are you going to do about it?"

Chapter TEN

Crownpoint is windy. Exceptionally windy. It is the kind of wind that inspires clichés: it really is chilling, regardless of the season; it truly does howl. The Diné have stories they tell about what kind of beings come out at night, and when I lived in Crownpoint I believed every word of those stories, because while the daytime wind had a magic to it, at night the wind reminded me that I was scared and alone and a thousand miles from home.

My WPA bunker turned apartment was just a football field away from Crownpoint Elementary, a U-shaped building shellacked with dozens of layers of paint, each one evidence of a custodian's furtive attempt to cover up fifth-graders' initial forays into the fine art of vulgar graffiti. The school anchored a corner of Crownpoint's busiest intersection. Its neighbors were the perennially busy Mustang gas station with the rip-off Taco Bell take-out window (Eddie Pepper's, home to an extremely serviceable bean burrito) and a makeshift flea market, where vendors would hawk pottery and spare parts and fatty hunks of barbecued mutton.

The final weeks of August were a blur of human resource trainings, panic attacks, and comedically ineffective attempts to decorate my classroom. In addition to leaving an absolute horror show of detritus for me to clean up, the previous occupant of room 33 had painted over a full wall of windows facing the school's courtyard playground. I spent hours scraping off the paint, pulling all-nighters in my classroom for a week but only truly succeeding in making a mess.

And then it was September. I put on Colin's old Dockers and one of my father's bright ties, stood at the front of my half-put-together classroom, and introduced myself to twenty or so appropriately skeptical preadolescents.

I struggled to describe my students to friends and family outside of Crownpoint. I wanted to neither whitewash everything that made them unique nor feed into myths about Native kids on the reservation. The truth was, my students were like every fifth-grader I had ever met, but they also lived in the country that conquered their people, stole their land, and massacred their ancestors. They played *Tony Hawk's Pro Skater* on their older siblings' PlayStations, left Flamin' Hot Cheetos fingerprints all over our classroom, and laughed at jokes about poop and farts, but they also played Diné string games in winter, attended ceremonies with their parents, and tried to frighten each other with skinwalker stories.

I invented my own metrics to prove that I wasn't a White savior. I took pride in being the first teacher at school and the last one with their light on at night. My bleary eyes were proof that I must be doing something right.

I longed for, and subsequently took immense pride in receiving, compliments from the most universally admired teacher in school, Ms. Begay, a veteran Navajo educator whom all the students adored. After months of asking Ms. Begay for advice, the day she mentioned that she liked the way I facilitated reading groups sent me to the moon. Would Ms. Begay of all people compliment a White savior? Of course not!

I sought a slightly different type of reassurance from my relationships with the TFA teachers I came down with, roughly forty other recent college graduates who were now scattered around tiny towns like Crownpoint. I loved our crew. But I also loved the idea that if I was one of them, I wasn't a colonist. They all had *Bury My Heart at Wounded Knee* on their shelves, they too were working hard at night, and they too had misgivings about what we were doing here. None of them were Navajo, but at least they weren't all White, and at least the ones who were White weren't the kind of White people I'd feared they'd be. If there were prep school elitists in our ranks, they at least hid it well.

But it still wasn't enough to cast away the doubts. Some days I walked home to my public works project apartment, feeling like I had completely nailed it because the kids learned place value, aced their spelling quizzes, and taught me a new word in Navajo. Other days, I made stupid rookie mistakes, the kind of unforced errors that a veteran teacher would know to avoid.

One afternoon while helping another student, I left an entire box of chalk open within easy reach of my biggest class clown, Tyler. It didn't take Tyler a full minute to first snap most of the pieces in half, then cover his entire face in a thick white mask, running from table to table, terrorizing his classmates with ghost sounds. Previous to becoming a teacher, I would have assumed that "preventing chalk-based ghost cosplay" would be an easy bar to clear. And yet . . .

Fortunately, as was the case back in high school, I had a set of foils here: less impressive White people to whom I could compare myself favorably. Crownpoint's other teachers were, in my and my TFA friends' telling, White outcasts who couldn't get jobs in Oklahoma. Though I didn't have much direct evidence to back up my assumption that these other White teachers were lazy, I assumed they were. While I walked in the front door with project-based learning lessons and other fancy tricks I heard about in my alternative certification classes, they printed off rote worksheets in the copy room right before class.

I convinced myself that these teachers were outwardly racist, though my evidence was largely apocryphal. Some of the older TFAers in town told me that a few years ago, there was a first-grade teacher who built a play church in her classroom because, as the story went, she believed "since they'll never amount to anything in this life, I might as well save their souls."

If the play-church teacher really existed, I never met her. But that didn't keep me from repeating the story, especially to friends and family in other parts of the country. "Thank God you're there," my friends would tell me. "Oh, I'm not the teacher my students really deserve," I'd reply. And I'd mean it, but I'd also smile.

Had I been curious, I could have been open to another story. But I didn't want to be curious about these other White teachers. If I offered them even the smallest bit of grace, there was the risk that I would have discovered something humanizing about them. It was so much easier to assume that they were racist, that they were dumb, that unlike me they had never gone to a powwow or signed a petition to free Leonard Peltier.

I tried not to be standoffish. I came to the faculty potlucks and made small talk in the teachers' lounge. But it was perfunctory. A lot of those White Okie teachers gave me gifts when I first moved into town. A table. Pots and pans. Even an old antenna TV—a hulking 1970s model, framed in dark wood, capable on a good wind day of picking up KOAT 7, the ABC affiliate out of Albuquerque. They made me dinner. They gave me teaching tips. Though I always said thank you, I can't remember giving any gifts in return.

I knew that many of these teachers were Republican (there were a few BUSH-CHENEY bumper stickers in the parking lot). Besides that, though, my only ammunition for establishing that these were different White people from me was all class judgments.

One second-grade teacher used to be a long-haul trucker. Many others worked blue-collar jobs. Other than the gym teacher, who was young and went to Oklahoma State, none of them attended their state's flagship universities. They went to community colleges, branch campuses, directional schools.

When payday came, the Okies ate at the Old Country Buffet in Gallup. My friends and I drove to Albuquerque to hang out in cool downtown bars like Anodyne, places that flattered my tastes with walls lined with books and a jukebox full of songs by the Minutemen and Joy Division. We went to college straight out of high school and often weren't the first in our family to do so. We always planned on working white-collar jobs. We wouldn't say it out loud, but many of us considered teaching a step down from so many paths that we could have taken.

I could have asked the Oklahoma teachers more about their pathway to the classroom—why they decided to leave the factory, a career on the open road, or a previous life as a stay-at-home mom. About what made them attend the hiring fairs that the perennially understaffed Gallup-McKinley County School District held back in their home state. What their connection to Native America was. A long history of intermarriage and cultural mixing meant that in Oklahoma, it's not uncommon for tribal members to be White-passing. So it's fair to say that at least some of those teachers, whom I just assumed were all White, had more of a connection to Indigenous America than I did. I never asked about any of that, though. I just filled in the gaps with the narrative that would silence my self-doubt.

What I didn't consider was that maybe the Okies had a story about me too.

My birthday is on March 9, deep in the pre–spring break doldrums of the school calendar. During my first year in Crownpoint, March 9 fell on a Monday. At the time, I was struggling to integrate Damion, a new student who had already been kicked out of two schools for violent outbursts. That morning, Damion crashed into my room with a fury, knocking over desks, flipping chairs, and yelling, "Nobody mess with me today; I shot my cousin this weekend."

Thinking quickly, I motioned Damion to join me in the hall. I spotted the music teacher, Mrs. Tompkins, walking toward my room. Mrs. Tompkins and her husband were two of the White Okies; he taught third grade and was usually the teacher with whom I secretly competed to be first in the building. When I first got to town, I took them up on their offers to join them for Sunday dinner or Friday bonfires, but as time went on I started flaking, until eventually the invitations dried up. Today, at least, I needed her help.

Fortunately, Mrs. Tompkins innately understood the situation. We tagged off, and I hustled my whirling dervish of a potential attempted-murder-committing student down the hallway. I didn't know what to do next, nor did I know how to react when we turned the corner and nearly ran right into my friend Kyle's first-graders, who, at that very moment, were marching down the hall to sing "Happy Birthday" to me. I rushed past them, attempting to explain the situation to Kyle with a blur of hand gestures and blubbered apologies. I tried not to notice the look of dejection on twenty previously bubbly seven-year-old faces.

Eventually, Damion and I rounded the corner and could finally talk. I thought I'd have to start the conversation, but a momentarily placid Damion took the wheel instead.

"What's the big deal? Why'd we have to come down here?"

"Damion, you just said you shot your cousin!"

"Oh, that?" he replied with a shrug. "It was just a BB gun."

When I returned to my classroom, Mrs. Tompkins glared at me, a complete one-eighty from her previous demeanor. It was impossible to ignore, but I was more than happy to just chalk it up to a character flaw on her part and continue teaching.

The morning went by uneventfully. I taught and then took my students to Mrs. Tompkins's portable classroom for music class. When I picked them up for lunch, I waited longer than usual. Much longer than usual. Long enough to get agitated.

In an elementary school, time is a precious resource. Our kids had forty minutes for lunch and recess. That block was one of the few moments of downtime that I or Mrs. Tompkins enjoyed in a day, and even that was often carved up with ad hoc meetings or students who needed extra tutoring. Even colleagues who despised each other respected one another's lunch blocks.

After fifteen minutes, my kids marched out, staring daggers at me. The last kid in line deposited a huge packet of papers in my hands and muttered something about how because of me, they wouldn't get recess. Hustling my kids along,

I heard a few of them cursing me under their breath. When we got into the building, all the other fifth-grade classes were lining up to go outside. The grumbles from my students got louder. I negotiated with the school cooks; they too cursed me under their breath. Finally, thoroughly confused as to how I had become public enemy number one so quickly, I retreated to my classroom, closed the door, and turned my attention to the pile of papers my student had shoved in my face after exiting Mrs. Tompkins's classroom.

They were essays, of sorts, each one with the same title, clearly copied off Mrs. Tompkins's chalkboard: "HOW I FEEL NOW THAT I KNOW THAT MR. BUCKS WAS DISRESPECTING ALL THE PEOPLE WHO DIED."

Goddamn it. This was about the Pledge of Allegiance. Mrs. Tompkins had been in my room when my students hadn't stood. They must have told her that I didn't make them stand. Here I was with my long hair and my liberal arts degree. Of course I was the kind of America hater who disrespected the military. Mrs. Tompkins loved and respected our troops, but so did our students. Many of my kids' family members were serving in Iraq at that time, as was at least one of Mrs. Tompkins's children. I picked up one of the papers and stared at an underlined sentence in the middle of the page.

"I come from a Warrior Clan. The Navajo have many warrior clans, and if Mr. Bucks doesn't like that he can go back to whatever country he's from."

Goddamn it!

I tried to find Mrs. Tompkins in the cafeteria. I desperately wanted to explain that this was just a misunderstanding. In college, I converted to Quakerism, and Quakers don't take oaths of any kind, nor do we require others to. *Let your ayes be ayes and your nays be nays.* I hoped to tell her about how I too was just trying to respect the people who died. "Mary Dyer, Quaker, Hanged on Boston Common—1660." Surely she'd understand.

Mrs. Tompkins was sitting by herself at one of those long, foldable metal cafeteria tables. Lunch service was done for the day, so other than my recess-deprived students on the other end of the room, it was just her, finishing her food as fast as possible. Leading with what I hoped was an appropriately nonthreatening request, I approached her.

"Mrs. Tompkins, I think there might have been a misunderstanding . . ."

She held up her hand. *"Garrett, no."*

"But it really isn't what it looked—"

"Garrett, no."

My students were staring at us now. I looked back to Mrs. Tompkins, who said nothing more but glared at me with the same intensity she had that morning. There was nothing I could do. I turned around and, as my kids continued to watch, slunk out the back of the cafeteria.

Eventually our principal, Ms. Jenkins—a gruff, no-nonsense Oklahoman herself who had successfully earned the loyalty of both our school's Okie redneck and TFA hippie contingents—brokered a hesitant peace deal.

"Mr. Buuuucks," she wheezed at me in her two-pack-a-day red-dirt drawl, "so, like, this was all a religious thing?"

"Yes, I'm Quaker, you see, and—"

"Yeah, whatever. Listen, I don't know how your whole deal works, but you're not gonna, like, go to hell if your kids say the pledge and you just, like, stand there silently, right?"

"I mean, I guess not."

"Good, well, that's settled then. And, Mrs. Tompkins, can you please do us all a favor and quit with this shit?"

Though she agreed to our boss's truce, Mrs. Tompkins shot me one last glare. Two days later, she came into my classroom in the morning to apologize to me in front of my students.

"I wanted you all to know that I have chosen to forgive Mr. Bucks, but he now understands the implications of what he did thanks to your essays."

For the rest of the year, the two of us did our best to avoid each other.

I tried even harder to be a model teacher, to prove that *I* was the one who belonged there. I learned Navajo phrases and taped a poster of Chief Manuelito on my wall. I tutored Damion after class to help him get caught up from the time he had missed ping-ponging to and from schools. I applied for grants to get our school fancy new computer equipment.

Visitors from TFA and the school district came into my classroom and marveled at my students' engagement and joy. I was chosen as one of our region's two nominees for TFA teacher of the year. Even Ms. Jenkins, not one to shower anybody with praise, said that I was one hell of a teacher.

All the while, Kjersti's and my relationship successfully carried on at a distance—Crownpoint to Guadeloupe the first year, Crownpoint to Chicago, where she was working in a University of Chicago microbiology lab, in the second. We were done living apart, though; we were mutually exhausted from trying to cram our life with each other into letters, mixtapes, long-distance phone calls, and the rare weekend when one of us had saved up enough money to afford a plane ticket.

While I had been trying to prove that I belonged in Crownpoint, Kjersti was deciding whether she was going to pursue a medical degree or a PhD in microbiology. One thing she knew for certain was that she wanted to live in Sweden before she officially chose one path over the other. While Kjersti had grown up in Idaho, Sweden was where she felt most fully herself. Her hometown of Pocatello was a Missoula-sized college town, but that's where the similarities ended. Pocatello was a majority Mormon town. Her family moved there because her father got a job teaching physics at Idaho State, but both he and Kjersti's mom were midwestern Lutherans turned liberal Unitarians. When she was growing up, Kjersti and her sister were frequently "gifted" the Book of Mormon from friends, each time with the insinuation that if they didn't convert, they'd end up in hell.

Kjersti's world changed in fifth grade. Her father took a sabbatical posting at Lund University, a classic Gothic campus in the south of Sweden. Lund was everything that Pocatello wasn't. Everybody knew how to pronounce her name. Her Swedish as a second language class was filled with kind, curious classmates from around the world. Nobody talked about religion. Kids were allowed to be kids, but in the best possible sense: getting free rein of their college town on bicycles and the city bus system. She felt seen and trusted as a girl in a way that had never been possible in Pocatello, where girls are taught at a young age that their sole role in life is to find a husband and gift the world an army of Mormon babies.

Kjersti loved Sweden and wanted to go back. I loved Kjersti and didn't want our relationship to end. We hatched a plan: we both applied for Fulbright fellowships in Stockholm and then crossed our fingers.

Crownpoint's squat little post office, another midcentury government relic, was directly to the south of my teacherage. Every day in the spring of 2005, I made a beeline for my mailbox as soon as school let out. The day I finally got word from the Fulbright Program, I ripped open the envelope right there in the post office's lobby and shrieked so loudly that the USPS employees at the front desk physically recoiled.

I sprinted home in a blur of tears, hurdled the fence outside my teacherage, and punched Kjersti's number into my phone. She answered immediately. Before I could even get the sentence out, both of us were shrieking and crying together. I then waited for the hour it took Kjersti to take a bus and two trains from Hyde Park on the South Side to her apartment in northwest Chicago. More envelope ripping, another phone call, more shrieking, more crying. Kjersti and I were going to make it. But that meant leaving Crownpoint.

I dreaded telling my students and hated that they weren't

shocked. I wasn't the first White man to come to New Mexico, make big promises, and leave. I also dreaded telling my principal, who wished me well but also reminded me that this was why she hesitated to hire TFAers.

Of all the conversations, the one with my parents was the toughest. They never asked me to apply for a Fulbright or chase prestige. They didn't care about how TFA was a big-name selective program either. They just loved visiting me in Crownpoint. And they were afraid in the best parental way that things wouldn't work out between Kjersti and me.

I was ashamed about what I thought leaving proved about me: I really was just a missionary. I cared about this town when it could make me feel better about myself, when I could get accolades for "the great thing I was doing for those kids," but as soon as a shiny, prestigious object was dangled in front of my eyes, I leaped for it.

On the last day of my second and final year teaching at Crownpoint, a kid scrawled FUCK MR. BUCKS on the playground slide. My kids and I had just had a big celebration of their increased test scores and demonstrably higher reading proficiencies. We hugged, watched *Spider-Man 2*, and ate dessert.

"With great power comes great responsibility," I told them between mouthfuls of grocery store sheet cake. A cheesy sentiment, but they were kind enough to not roll their eyes. We cried and hugged and more than a few of them told me that I was their favorite teacher.

I thought I nailed the perfect goodbye. But then I walked

outside and there was the Sharpied counterpoint for all the world to see.

I don't know if the "Fuck Mr. Bucks" was written by a student who was angry at me for leaving or angry at me for coming in the first place. I tried wiping off that graffiti, but it wouldn't come out. So I scribbled over it, packed up my apartment, and left town.

PART THREE

Church
and State
(Interlude)

Chapter ELEVEN

When I was born, Eric, Colin, Brian, and Nate were twelve, eleven, nine, and six, respectively. They were, with very few exceptions, uncommonly kind to me. Dan and Jane Bucks raised us to be kind to one another. I was also so much younger than they were, so picking on me was more cruel than satisfying. But I do remember two distinct moments when they made me angry. The first was when they tried to scare me by throwing one of my mother's chickens at me, yelling, "They'll peck you and you'll get chicken pox!" The second was when they came into my room and turned the cardboard portraits I had hanging above my bed upside down.

The cardboard cutouts were of George Washington and Abraham Lincoln. I proudly placed them above my bed because, well . . . I couldn't imagine why anybody wouldn't. If my bed was the only space that was singularly and truly mine (as was the case in that house full of Bucks children, foster babies, and—in the coldest months—even our chickens, whom my mother boarded in the laundry room), of course I would use that space to pay tribute to the most important people in American history. And of course those tributes should be right side up.

The two cutouts were not equal in my heart. Washington was a fairly perfunctory choice. I honored him mostly because he was the first president.

It was Lincoln who really earned that spot, though. I knew only three facts about Lincoln, but those three facts were deeply meaningful. First, I knew that he had guided America through the Civil War, and as a child who hated wars, I was grateful he cleaned up that mess before I came around. Second, I knew (or I assumed at least) that he was a White president who loved Black people. I mean, he must have loved Black people, right? That's why he freed them from slavery. Third, he was born in a log cabin, which is to say that he was born somewhere remote and unimportant, but he had made his way to somewhere immensely important. He wasn't from Clancy, Montana, but he might as well have been from Clancy, Montana.

I spent a lot of time in the living room with a road atlas in those days, tracing the routes out of Clancy. Eric joked that I was plotting my getaway. I explained I wasn't trying to run away. I just needed to know how to get from Clancy to someplace important, someplace that would make my life meaningful. I always started the same way, tracing Interstate 15 from Clancy down to the L.A. metro area. That's where White boys met beatific aliens. Then I hopped to the other important cities.

New York made the list, it being, of course, the location that the Muppets took in *The Muppets Take Manhattan*, as did Chicago, because my brothers let me watch *Ferris Bueller's Day Off* with them if I didn't tell my mother. The only non-cinematic location I chose was, naturally, Washington, D.C.

When Barack Obama was elected president in 2008, I overheard a couple of coworkers of color joke about whether, up to this moment, little White boys looked at all the White male presidents and automatically assumed that they would be president too. The answer for me was, without equivocation, yes.

It wasn't that I grew up thinking that I could be president. It's that I grew up feeling, without anybody telling me, that I was obligated to one day become known for being unimpeachably good. If that meant becoming president, then so be it.

Throughout my life, I told myself—always just myself, mind you, never out loud, for that would reveal me to be unbearably vainglorious—a story about heroes who were many steps closer to me than Lincoln. I told myself a story that I came from a place that produced heroes, but that the story of that heroism was unfinished. Year after year, I told myself a ghost story.

———

What's important to know about South Dakota is that once you drive west across the Missouri River, the state is quite striking. That half of the state includes the sacred Black Hills and the otherworldly Badlands. It is home to lush conifer forests and vast subterranean caves. There are buffalo and pronghorns, waterfalls and canyons, peaks and valleys. South Dakota is exactly half a state of delight and wonder.

All of that—the variety, the grandeur, the contrast—stops on a dime on the banks of the Missouri. It is impossible to describe the eastern half of South Dakota except by chronicling that which it isn't. It's the desert before the oasis. It's the life sentence before the commutation. It is flat. Pancake flat. Two-dimensionally flat. The product of grand geologic forces happening *around it*: mountains rising to its west, wind erosion spilling the dust across the prairie, scorching-hot summers and arctic winters discouraging anything more rootless than acres upon acres of prairie grass from finding sustenance. It is the easiest place in the world to build a highway system. There are barely any obstacles to dodge. Just straight lines toward the horizon, forever.

None of this is an insult, by the way. East River, South Dakota, is magical, though in an entirely different way from the mountainous West River. A flatness that complete and all-encompassing isn't a curse. It's a gift, a challenge, a canvas. It is an invitation shouted across the prairie: this place will be as beautiful or as cruel, as imaginative or as depraved, as the creatures who occupy it.

It is, for instance, the ideal combination of flora, fauna, and topography for the ring-necked pheasant, a species that, by all accounts, loves eastern South Dakota more than any other location on the planet. The pheasants don't complain about the lack of mighty cedar trees or breathtaking desert mesas or roaring rivers. This place has always been their home, and that's enough.

Human beings are different from pheasants, though. At least I like to think we are. The places where we live, particularly ones as open to interpretation as eastern South Dakota, can become heaven, hell, or everything in between. That was true when the first groups of Mound Builders made their way here. That was true when various bands of Arikara and Dakota came and went and came again. That was true when the U.S. government passed the Homestead Act and dispatched the U.S. Calvary to either move or kill any Natives who might disagree with having their land taken. And that was true when railroad tracks were laid and towns and cities full of White people started popping up on the prairie.

If being human in the West means the ability to have a hometown to call your own, to never have your American family tree cut short by genocide, to have your western story be an epic romance rather than an unspeakable tragedy, then Doland exists because the United States of America believed in my humanity more than that of the Indigenous people who trace their roots to that same patch of flat land east of the Missouri River. Doland is a place where my ancestors were given the right to create their own version of heaven, but only after other White people first scorched the earth and made it hell.

There's a reason I've clung to the idea of Doland as a place whose legacy needed to be reclaimed. There's a reason I was obsessed with the idea of that town and towns like it as being places that once created great (male) progressive heroes. Because if Doland, South Dakota, could produce Hubert Humphrey and Mitchell, South Dakota, could produce George McGovern and Orient, Iowa, could produce Henry Wallace—each of them, at one time or another, standard-bearers for the dream of egalitarian social democracy in the United States, all three of them at one point both very close and very far away from the presidency—then perhaps not just these places, but my American story, might be redeemable.

And so I am haunted by Doland. I'm haunted by what created Doland and therefore what created me. I'm haunted by the story I still cling to about what Doland could have been and could have given the world. I'm haunted by the way in which that dream ceased to be, how towns like Doland stopped both producing and voting for politicians who appealed to their better angels and followed the rest of rural White America in the direction of increasingly reactionary messengers and messages.

There's a complicated, multifaceted narrative about how all that happened. It's a story of bankrupted farms, busted unions, and fewer close social bonds. It's a story of successful appeals to reactionary boogeymen: anticommunism and "law and order" and whispers that the Blacks and the Natives were getting too uppity. It's also a story of sorting and peacocking—of college-educated Whites increasingly gravitating to places like Columbia and Missoula and non-college-educated Whites staying in places like Clancy and Doland, of both groups distancing themselves from each other but needing the other as a reminder of what they are not. And, of course, it's a story about small towns never truly welcoming so many people who might have wanted to make a home there—people of color, queer people, women, broke people, all sorts of people.

It's not a story that could have been resolved by singular great White men, be they Abraham Lincoln or Hubert Humphrey or even Ken Gelston. But I wanted so badly to believe that I was the next Great White Hope.

Chapter TWELVE

There was another story, though. A road not taken. Exactly a decade before I left for Sweden with Kjersti, I dreamed of being a Methodist pastor. The dream was born the summer after my freshman year of high school, an hour north of Missoula. I was at Flathead Lake United Methodist Church Camp. There was the fire, the semicircle of seats, and the lanky, rustic cross: two skinny branches that were somehow strong enough to stay upright in the face of the considerable gusts that blew in from the lake.

The message from our cool, hacky-sack-playing, college-aged counselors was that thanks to our faith in God and the support of our community, we could accomplish anything we set our minds to. This was news to me, since that week I had failed to convince various girls from Belgrade and Great Falls and Helena to make out with me. But that night, the weather-beaten cross in front of that glacier-fed lake and the warm, hopeful faces of my friends peering through the campfire smoke all did their trick. We sang "Sanctuary" accompanied by acoustic guitars, and I ran my fingers idly over a freshly gifted hemp necklace, and I felt both incredibly warm and incredibly cold at the same time. I cried and was immediately smothered in accepting teenage hugs. I knew what all this meant. I knew that God was in those hugs.

When I was growing up, the United Methodist Church was a classic big-tent White Protestant denomination. Like all Methodist sects, its roots were in the teachings of John Wesley, an English theologian and evangelist who asserted that all people have the free will to choose salvation, which in turn was found through both faith in God and righteous deeds on earth.

In many southern states, being a Methodist basically meant that you were part of your town's White aristocracy. Nice, upper-class White folks went to the Methodist Episcopal church while Black folks attended the African Methodist Episcopal church across town. Although John Wesley had been an outspoken abolitionist, Methodism became one more tool to reinforce existing caste structures.

In the American West, though, Methodism had its roots in a small group of legendary circuit-riding preachers who traveled from town to town delivering sermons to farmers, loggers, and miners. Western Methodism was iconoclastic, less bound to hierarchy and more open to radical ideas. It was the kind of fertile, theologically curious soil that was ready-made for the Social Gospel, a progressive theological movement that emerged in the nineteenth and early twentieth centuries with the message that the Church's role was to challenge racial and class caste systems and offer comfort to those on the edges of society.

If you asked me as a child what it meant to be a Methodist, I would have talked about the endless calendar of potlucks: night after night of gatherings in linoleum-tiled basements where our mother directed us not to rush to the front of the line to raid the bucket of Kentucky Fried Chicken and instead let others go ahead of us, even if this meant that all the chicken and lemon bars would be gone and we'd have to fill our plates with *Diet for a Small Planet*–inspired grain casseroles.

When my family moved to Maryland, we couldn't find the nonstop-potluck energy we had coveted at St. Paul's. Columbia's Methodist churches felt more like generic clock-in, clock-out spiritual rest stops that families patronized in between weekends filled with lacrosse games and dance recitals: arrive, listen to a preacher tell you that God is good, sing a few hymns, walk to the front of the church to receive a hunk of grocery store bread and Welch's grape juice for communion, shake hands, and go home. They were fine, these churches. They just weren't for us.

Now theologically homeless, my parents temporarily abandoned Methodism for a lovely little church: a co-op of sorts comprising three liberal-ish Protestant denominations that met in one of James Rouse's beloved interfaith centers. We enjoyed that community, but we always had one foot out the door. We weren't really Congregationalists, Brethren, or Disciples of Christ. We were Montana Methodists in exile.

Because our move to Missoula occurred right as I started

high school, that meant Missoula First United Methodist Church would be the first religious home that I attended not out of obligation but of my own free will. When my brothers hit high school, my parents were less strict with their church attendance. They all had jobs and extracurriculars, sufficient justification to skip out on organized religion. I had those same excuses, but when that offer of spiritual emancipation came for me, I didn't take it. I loved church! I had always loved it! People were kind to our family there! People seemed to respect me there!

In my adult life, I've met hundreds of friends and acquaintances for whom growing up in the church was a source of trauma, judgment, and alienation. Church was a place where teen girls were humiliated and queer people were told they didn't belong. And while Montana Methodism was a human creation, and therefore a fallible space where the power dynamics of our small towns and cities could of course come to roost, Montana Methodism was, more often than not, also a respite from the world outside of church doors, especially for its youth.

Less than six months after returning to Montana, I was spending my weekends sleeping on church floors in Billings, Great Falls, and Bozeman and meeting kids who were simultaneously completely normal (there was the full range of letter-jacketed jocks, *Magic: The Gathering*–obsessed nerds, glassy-eyed stoners, and belt-buckled farm kids that you'd find in any Montana high school) but also not.

Back in our high schools, we were no different from our

peers—as self-conscious and selfish and cruel and judgmental as any other teenagers. Here, though, unbound by the social hierarchies that dominated our weekdays, we were kinder, more curious, and less cliquey. There were far fewer things to compete for here; there were no automatic blessings bestowed on those who could run faster, jump higher, or understand calculus better. We were allowed to be beautiful to one another.

We'd gather in those church halls and listen to liberal Montana youth ministers deliver messages about love (for God, for one another, for the world), and then we'd sing goofy praise songs, always aided by a small army of dudes who had hauled their acoustic guitars across the state for the occasion. There were even hand motions, those great enemies of teenage vanity.

We'd sing, *"He came from hea-ven to earth,"* and bring our hands first up as high as possible and then down to an imagined plateau in front of us. A few lines later, we'd belt out, *"From the cro-oosss to the grave / From the grave to the sky,"* and there we all were, first holding up a cross in front of us and then pretending to *literally dig a grave for Jesus.* And all that, somehow, was not ridiculous. All that was safe for the jocks and the stoners and the debate champions to do all at once. All that somehow made me like and trust the others.

I attended my first statewide Methodist youth conference over Presidents' Day weekend in 1996. I piled into a car with three other kids from Missoula First United and drove east through a Montana February, the dirty snow month, the single period in the western calendar that never inspires any paeans to its beauty.

But when we walked into the light-filled sanctuary at Bozeman United Methodist Church, the murk disappeared. Everybody was happy to see us, to see *me*, even though I had given them no reason to. Midway through the weekend, I learned two important pieces of information. The first was that if I wanted to repeat this experience in the summer, I could attend camp on Flathead Lake. The second was that all this was planned by a statewide council—something you could run for and be elected to. I jumped at both chances. That summer at camp brought the gift of that skinny cross and, with it, a professional and spiritual direction for the rest of my life. Statewide elected office, in turn, gave way to invitations to national conferences, and before I knew it the Methodist Church was not just subsidizing my Trailways bus trips across the state, but flights to Tennessee for national Methodist youth council meetings.

Those meetings taught me that, in some ways, Montana Methodists *were* different from the Church as a whole. The kids who came from White congregations in the South and Midwest had a greater comfort in big churches with praise bands and much less comfort in the idea that the Church should be okay with gay kids.

My first national council meeting was in August 1997, the summer after my sophomore year. Thirty or so of us from across the country slept on cots in the attic of McKendree United Methodist Church in downtown Nashville.

McKendree didn't look like the humble but welcoming frontier church buildings back home. It was a white-pillared Old
South citadel, its fortressness a deliberately buffered contrast
to the sin-filled honky-tonks of nearby Broadway.

We spent our days brainstorming plans for future national
youth gatherings in the nondescript, fluorescent-lit church office
buildings across the street from Vanderbilt University, taking a
break for lunch at the various undergraduate-focused fast-food
joints on 21st Avenue. I remember getting Burger King one afternoon with Trent, a blond kid from Texas. We sat on the front
patio, the sun melting the ice in my fountain Coke as we ate our
Double Whoppers, and Trent talked about why he was a Chris-
tian in a language that was foreign to me. I nodded along as
he mentioned "saving souls" and "a personal relationship with
Jesus Christ," and then, when it was my turn to testify, I fiddled
with my fries, not really knowing what to say, mumbling something about how beautiful the sunset looks over Flathead Lake.

For all the differences, though, these national spaces also
offered me everything that kept me rushing back to my own
youth group back home. At night, in McKendree's cavernous
attic, we played Mafia for hours and traded CDs back and
forth—Mary J. Blige and the Notorious B.I.G. traveling from
Black hands to White, Garth Brooks and Green Day traveling
from White to Black.

All this was happening in the 1990s, a time when mainline, majority White Protestantism—represented by denominations like the Methodists, Presbyterians, Lutherans, and
Episcopalians—was deeply concerned that it was dying.

For the first half of the twentieth century, these big-tent Protestant denominations drew the bulk of their congregants from the liberal to center-right political spectrum. They benefited from an era when White America's politics were moderated by New Deal affluence, high union participation, and relatively few outward challenges to racial hierarchies. Starting in the 1970s, though, the White mainline churches saw a precipitous decline in membership. While some of that decline was attributable to the country's diversification, it also represented the shifting politics of American Whiteness after the civil rights movement of the 1960s.

Just as the late twentieth and early twenty-first centuries saw White communities, particularly White working-class communities, increasingly throw their political support behind candidates like George Wallace, Ronald Reagan, and Donald Trump, so too did the moderate to conservative wing of the mainline denominations find itself attracted to the "traditional values" of megachurch Evangelicalism.

Since these changes were rooted in sociological patterns beyond the purview of denominational policy, mainline Protestant institutions grasped at straws as they saw their pews grow emptier and emptier. While I didn't know any of the broader context at the time, I benefited directly from that uncertain moment, for in the 1990s, there was no shortage of free money for any teenagers willing to raise their hands and declare that they wanted to be mainline Protestant preachers.

This is all to say, none of our stories occurs in a vacuum, and there was context as to why, in 1998, the Lilly Endowment, the large Indianapolis-based pharmaceutical philanthropy, paid my way to spend an entire summer at a theology institute at Emory University in Atlanta.

That summer, cocooned in Emory's Italian Renaissance campus, I met White kids from the Chicago suburbs and Cuban kids from Miami and Black kids from Dallas and Asian kids from Seattle, all of whom, like me, wondered whether we were the only teenager out there who was politically left wing *and* who really wanted to be a pastor. We were delighted to have found one another, to discover that we were somehow not the only ones out there living in the middle of that hyperspecific Venn diagram. It felt like a miracle, so of course we sought out more evidence of the miraculous around us. We knew this experience together was fun, but we wanted it to be something more than that. We wanted it to be holy. We knew that we were accepted by one another, but was it too much to have that acceptance also be officially affirmed by God?

But here's the thing about faith and religion: it is impossible—for me at least, and I assume for others who believe in God—to know where otherworldly holiness stops and our biases and insecurities begin. We all draw our own map of the border between the sacred and the profane. This is one of the reasons this whole Christianity business has always been a mess of contradictions. It's why, not long after its founding, it was the home base for both the empire and its discontents, for the slaver, slave, and abolitionist alike. So, when teenage me sat by that campfire and felt an intense, cocooning warmth, how could I know for sure that I was experiencing an omnipotent God personally telling me that they had special plans for me? What if the more obvious explanation was true: that the love I felt that night had more to do with nonjudgmental community than divine intervention?

The second answer could have been enough. It could have been a lovely lesson. And that alone could have led me to a career in the ministry.

But I wanted it to be the first answer. I wanted so badly to know that in that moment God, the creator of the universe and all that was holy, had directed all their godly force to a tiny bonfire in northwest Montana and singled out a gangly, pale-in-spite-of-a-summer-outdoors teenager for divine duty.

I wasn't the only kid prone to self-aggrandizement that summer. The theology institute was full of bold declarations about the designs that God had for our teenage lives.

It wasn't enough to just have a crush on somebody in a space such as this. Instead, we'd send mash notes back and forth to each other about how "what God has put together, let no man pull apart." Nor were our other preoccupations ever solely our own.

My roommate Dave was from Texas, the son of Korean immigrants. We stayed up late, talking with equal passion about our romantic entanglements and our hopes for the future, two topics that he had fully figured out. God wanted him to marry his girlfriend, a competitive dancer from his hometown, and was also "calling" him to apply to Princeton.

One evening, over a dinner of chicken tenders and fries in the cafeteria, I nodded as a crowd of girls hatched a plan to tell their mothers, upon returning home, that "because God is a woman and she's a feminist," they weren't shaving their legs anymore.

It was silly and sweet all at once, which is to say that it *was*, in fact, holy. We were self-important and overly earnest, but we were self-important and overly earnest together. I'm sure the divinity students who served as our instructors and pseudo camp counselors rolled their eyes at us, but I'm also sure they understood.

My final moment as a Montana Methodist was in 1999, the summer before I left for Earlham. For once I wasn't traveling the country on the Lilly Endowment dime. I was back at home with my fellow Yellowstone Conference attendees, kids I'd known since moving back to Montana. We gathered for a week of worship services and parliamentary meetings for adults and youth alike. There was a final worship service at First United Methodist Church in downtown Billings—the only space other than Flathead Lake where I experienced that quaking warmth that I interpreted as a calling.

There I was, sitting on a pew next to all my friends as the adults did various adult Methodist business in front of us. There was a small jumble of newly ordained preachers being recognized by the assembly before being sent off to Chinook or Plentywood or whichever small town would be their first charge. There was a hymnal in the pew in front of me, which I opened and immediately flipped to the back inner cover, as I did every time I sat down in any Montana Methodist church, searching for the one true assurance that I was home. There, taped in the back, was a song only we sang, one I taught to all my new friends across the country but knew didn't belong to them the way it belonged to us.

"Harvest Time" was written by W. A. Spencer, a nineteenth-century hymn composer from Rock Island, Illinois, just across the Mississippi from Vera and Russell Bucks's original Iowa farm. As a lyricist, Spencer had a flair for the dramatic and macabre. The song's original title was "The Seed I Have Scattered in Springtime with Weeping," a title at home in a Spencer catalog that also included "Companions in This Holy War" and "Go Tell the World Who Are Watching in Sorrow."

None of us Montana Methodists had any idea who W. A. Spencer was, so "Harvest Time" wasn't really Spencer's song to us. It was Brother Van's song. That's what it said on the top of all those pasted-in sheets of paper: "Harvest Time: Brother Van's Song." This was our origin story in verse, us Montana United Methodists. We were here, in our little Social Gospel churches, being nicer to one another than high schoolers are supposed to be, because a century previously, a pastor named William Wesley Van Orsdel rode around our state on horseback, planting churches everywhere he stopped.

"Harvest Time" has a jolting, discordant melody. It isn't particularly catchy, but I can't hear it sung chorally without collapsing into a puddle of tears. The song's primary message is that farming is awful and harrowing; you have to do all this work with no promise of profit, but there will be a harvest at some point, and you have to believe that the harvest will be worth it.

> *The seed I have scattered in springtime with weeping,*
> *And watered with tears and with dews from on high.*

It's not an uplifting message. The song rallies for a bit of hopefulness at the end, but just barely.

> *But the tears of the sower and the songs of the reaper*
> *Shall mingle together with joy by and by.*

There is slight relief in that single line, a final reminder that a farmer's tears will eventually turn to joy in that "*sweet by and by.*" It's a nice sentiment, until you realize that "the sweet by and by" means death. It's a dour anthem. But it's our dour anthem. And so I sat in that pew that summer day and looked first at my friends' earnest, pimpled faces and then back at that secret hymn that a kindly Montana Methodist pasted in our hymnals, and in that moment, all my ambition, duty, and guilt were gone. In its place I just felt immensely, completely, at home.

————

Later that day, my friends and I piled into a car and drove to a Fuddruckers for burgers. Somebody took Dave Matthews and Tim Reynolds's *Live at Luther College* out of a hulking black album of discs and put it on the car stereo. Soon the initial chords of "Crash into Me" filtered through the car, the exact kind of song that, were I with a group of kids I was trying to impress, I'd have claimed to hate. It was too treacly, too earnest, too popular. It wasn't punk. It wasn't challenging. It was an acoustic guitar dude crooning about sex in the corniest way possible.

In another setting, I would have rolled my eyes, but not here, not with friends for whom I didn't have to put on airs, not holding the hand of a teenage crush that this time was (finally!) requited and riding in a car to go eat burgers. Here I admitted that I loved this song, that I loved these people, that I wanted nothing more than to hold their hands forever.

Chapter THIRTEEN

I left Montana—temporarily, I told myself. I left for Earlham, the college I chose specifically because it offered me the one thing that the bigger, more prestigious schools where my fellow achievement-addicted peers were heading did not: the Quakerly promise of a port in the storm. In retrospect, I realize that I was hoping to reconcile my ambition and my deep desire for the comfort of nonjudgmental community. The ambitious, self-aggrandizing White boy version of myself—the one who was haunted by Doland and still envisioned a future where I would finish the job that Ken and Hubert couldn't—craved a college that was overtly political, overtly leftist, overtly righteous. Meanwhile, the part of me that had found a situationally less self-conscious home in church basements and attics—the me that had recently promised my God that I wouldn't immediately launch a political career and instead return to a tiny church in Montana—wanted to be around relatively egoless, kindhearted peers who would treat me like the kids in youth group did.

Even though Earlham was a place that I sought out in large part because I would be surrounded by as many people who shared my politics as possible, I still jostled and preened to ensure that, even in this space, I was unassailably on the right side of history. Those were the years of pretending to understand Derrida on the weekdays and dodging tear gas canisters on the weekend. They were the years of sometimes being vegetarian and then deriding the vegetarians and vegans for classism. They were the years when even my own kind, bleeding-heart father—not one to mock any of his children—laughed at how my transcript could be filled with a dozen courses with "gender" and "race" and "social construction of" in the title but no chemistry or English literature.

Officially, I didn't have any doubts about my pre-ministerial path all through college. My story remained the same. I was a socialist and a feminist and a traitor to Whiteness and an LGBTQ+ ally, but I was also going to be a pastor.

I may not have said I was wavering, but in retrospect the table was more than set for a single persuasive argument to shake me off my path. All it took was a single women's studies professor, an acerbic, straight-talking veteran of multiple waves of feminist activism named Bev (students at Earlham refer to their professors by their first names, both because of a Quakerly aversion to titles and because it was a piece of information the school could offer to prospective students as proof that it was "not like those other colleges"), to rattle my foundations.

Bev wasn't trying to curse her students with existential crises, mind you. She was just teaching feminist theory. But intentional or not, that's what happened in that classroom on the second floor of Carpenter Hall—a classroom that really did look like the undergraduate classrooms in movies, all aged wood and seats facing one another and chalkboards scrawled with riddles like SIGN DIVORCED FROM SIGNIFIER and ANTI–WORLD BANK PROTEST PLANNING MEETING POSTPONED. We were reading feminist theology. We were talking about the Council of Nicaea and goddess-centered religions. We were asking questions about the role of powerful leaders from long-lost empires in establishing Christ's divinity as settled fact.

Bev made a convincing argument.

If I was a true feminist (which of course I wanted to be; that's what Jane Bucks raised me to be) and if what I was learning about how the notion of Jesus's divinity was established by a group of men with an interest in making Christianity an imperialistic faith was true, then I couldn't believe that Jesus was literally God. If, in turn, I couldn't believe in the divinity of Christ, I couldn't preach in a Trinitarian church. And if I couldn't preach in a Trinitarian church, I couldn't be a Methodist minister anymore.

That was that. All through college, I continued to imagine the day I would return to Billings First United in pastoral vestments. I imagined the congregation singing "Harvest Time" and my old youth group friends hugging me, tears in our eyes. I imagined packing all my radical books into a box alongside my childhood Bible, placing them lovingly in the trunk of a car, and driving to my first church.

In that dream, I would have become a beloved part of a small town's life. I would have attended high school basketball games and eightieth birthday parties. I would have listened to a new generation of farmers and ranchers tell me how hard it was to make a living off the land, and then we would've sung "Harvest Time" together, and in that moment the ghosts of every Montana Methodist, from Brother Van forward, would've been there with us.

The most miraculous and anomalous part of the dream, of course, was that it was the only professional aspiration I ever held sustainably that was enough in and of itself. I didn't need to also become president or a Supreme Court justice. I didn't need to finish the job that Doland's heroes weren't able to. I didn't need an accomplishment to prove that all the love I had received in my life was worth it. I was just a small-town pastor. I was just a part of a community.

It was, in that way, the only vision for my life that I've ever had that was earnest and unselfconscious. It was this pure, less selfish anomaly in my life where I defined who I wanted to be in relationship to other people rather than out of a sweaty desire to prove my worthiness (as a White man layered in privilege, as a Bucks boy showered in familial love, as a one-generation-removed child of Doland).

The pastoral dream was always an outlier; it's a miracle I held on to it as long as I did.

The day I decided that my feminism precluded me from

joining the ministry, the dream stopped dead in its tracks. I stopped calling myself a Methodist and started calling myself a Quaker. It was a compromise position. I wasn't abandoning religion, but I was abandoning a religion whose ministers were expected to preach about a Triune god.

The Methodist Church went on without me. Over the next decade, it would do its best to prove that my decision to leave was the right one. Every year, that denomination's already tenuous big tent frayed a little bit more. The flash point was LGBTQ+ rights—whether our denomination would ordain gay pastors and perform gay weddings. The western and northeastern Methodists said yes. The southern and midwestern Methodists were more likely to say no, as were international Methodists, especially Methodists in Africa. By 2023, the old big-tent denomination finally split in two: the liberal churches remained United Methodists, while the conservative ones became Global Methodists.

Occasionally, my old pastoral aspirations would return, but less as an actual viable alternate life path and more like a somnambulant fantasy. Garrett Bucks daydreaming about being a pastor was now no different from Garrett Bucks, asleep, flying through the air. Each subsequent time it returned, the dream was a little bit gauzier, a little less real.

I knew that, objectively, there would have been very little romance or perfection in the ministerial path. The dream felt perfect only because it never became reality. Had I pursued the ministry, I would have found myself presiding over tiny, aging congregations, places where every death of a congregant brings the institution itself closer to its last days. The actual small towns I would have lived in wouldn't feel, to an adult with left-wing politics, like the utopian memories I had of Clancy School. I would have encountered bitterness and bigotry and conspiracy theories. Even in the 1990s, small towns around Missoula were hotbeds for wild-eyed antigovernment militias, long before the twenty-first century and the rise of Fox News and Trump and QAnon.

Moreover, I would likely not have found a pure, uncomplicated home in Methodism. I would have tuned in to the proceedings of various General Conferences only to have my heart break as my fellow pastors argued that Methodists shouldn't ordain gay preachers or take a stance on Black Lives Matter.

The road not taken wouldn't have been perfect. It might even have been terrible. But that doesn't mean that I don't mourn it.

PART FOUR

Exceptional, Alone

Chapter FOURTEEN

For Methodists, the confirmation process—the steps that one takes to officially become a member of the church—typically takes place sometime in the teenage years. In my case, that meant me and my youth group buddies spending a few Saturdays in 1997 gathered on folding chairs, listening to Missoula First United Methodist's pastor, Steve Garnaas-Holmes. A songwriter and a poet (he was one of the St. Paul's UMC-affiliated musicians who teamed up with Desmond Tutu), Pastor Steve was a minor star in progressive American Protestantism. He was charismatic and quippy, but also deeply philosophical.

Our class didn't have a rigid structure—Pastor Steve liked to riff—but it still built toward a crescendo of sorts. One day, while sitting on a back porch with a striking view of Missoula's protective ring of Rocky Mountain foothills, Steve delivered the only message we could tell he truly wanted us to remember.

"You know, you all, there are only two religions in the

world. The religion of being right and the religion of being in love. And the only rule is you're not allowed to be a member of both at the same time."

I nodded and affirmed to Steve that yes, I understood the profundity of what he'd said.

The problem was that there were two things that Pastor Steve didn't share when he dropped that koan into our laps. I don't blame him for the omission, mind you. Even if he had laid them out explicitly, I'm sure I still would have had to discover them for myself.

The first was how easy it was to lie to myself as to what religion—the being in love one or the being right one—I was choosing at any given point. "I'm not doing this for myself, I'm doing it because I just care so much" rolls off the tongue much easier than I assumed it would.

The second was that the religion of being right offers so many incredible perks. Rightness opens doors. Rightness may not silence fears, but it can drown them out for a while. Rightness may not replace phantom limbs, but it can provide the illusion that nothing was ever lost.

In *Minor Feelings*, her memoir about the dilemmas and dual consciousness of twenty-first-century Asian American identity, Cathy Park Hong writes about how much she hates the oft-repeated reductive racial truism that Asian Americans will be the next group assimilated into Whiteness. "When I hear the phrase 'Asians are next in line to be white,'" Hong writes, "I replace the word 'white' with 'disappear.' Asians are next in line to disappear. We are reputed to be so accomplished, and so law-abiding, we will disappear into this country's amnesiac fog."

I encountered *Minor Feelings* as a forty-year-old adult in 2021, during the second year of the COVID-19 pandemic. Reading that section alone in my bedroom sent a jolt of recognition through my body. *So that's why I've been so eager to prove that I am a worthy White person,* I thought.

I wanted to choose the religion of being in love, but the religion of being right offered something much more seductive.

Chapter FIFTEEN

The summer of 2006, I moved to Stockholm, a city of bridges, simple but elegant social democratic architecture, and cardamom-scented cinnamon rolls. Kjersti's and my Fulbright fellowships were generous—we received a year's worth of living stipend and the freedom to choose exactly how we filled or didn't fill our days. It was a rare gift, one that I regularly looked in the mouth.

I wasn't teaching that year. I was no longer on my feet all day, breaking up fights or watching eleven-year-olds discover their new favorite book. And because I wasn't in constant motion, I felt like my entire self had vanished. Just a few months previously, I had a classroom full of students and a chorus of voices around me assuring me that I was doing "such important work on the reservation." Now I was just one more pale blond nobody in a sea of pale blond humanity.

Faced with what felt like my own disappearance, I bolted in the opposite direction of the religion of love. I wanted to be right, as quickly as possible, specifically in comparison to all these Swedes around me.

My solution was to glom on to other international students, students of color specifically. I'd grab *dagens lunch* in the university restaurant with Diego from Argentina and Hua from Taiwan, and over plates piled high with baked salmon with dill sauce and boiled potatoes, they'd tell me, "Sweden's not actually a utopia, you know; it's quite racist—I can tell how people stare at me." I'd nod thoughtfully, not admitting that, to me, Sweden really had felt like a utopia. I hated that my classmates felt judged and unwelcome here. I earnestly wished that were not the case. But also . . . I loved knowing that I was the one they told. What a thrill, as a White person, learning about how terrible all the other White people are. What a terrific perk of the religion of being right.

When our Fulbrights ended, Kjersti and I moved to Chicago. I found a house with my two best friends from New Mexico. Our neighborhood had been Puerto Rican a couple of decades previously but was increasingly full of flat-faced fake brick condos. I'd ride my bike northwest up Milwaukee Avenue to the apartment Kjersti shared with a couple of other friends in a different neighborhood, one where the Puerto Rican families were just starting to leave, the construction crews swarming in to gut their houses and erect the fake brick.

I was teaching again, English as a second language for refugee adults. There was a whole new set of doubts. My students were decades older than me. They had lived entire lives in Myanmar, Colombia, and Eritrea. They were mothers and fathers. Professionals. I was twenty-five, wearing thrift store sweaters and spending most of my disposable income on concerts at the Empty Bottle and Schubas Tavern.

My students embarrassed me with their deference and gratitude. I'd teach them what the various columns on a hotel job application meant, and they'd look me in my eyes, grab my hand, and solemnly intone, "Teacher, thank you, for everything."

One of my students, Diallo from the Republic of the Congo, had been an award-winning muckraking journalist in his home country. He was so skilled and tenacious that the autocratic president Denis Sassou-Nguesso personally targeted him as an enemy of the state. But in a country where he didn't speak the language, none of that mattered. In Brazzaville, he was respected and feared. In the United States, he clothed his family in donations from the Lutheran churches in Wilmette and Palatine.

Diallo would talk to me for hours after class. He'd write me long letters about how angry he was about the war that had forced him here, as well as the disdain and pity he felt from Americans. He thanked me profusely for my presence in his life, but I suspected it was only because I had passed a low comparative bar in an uncaring place. I showed him more respect than the security guards at the *Chicago Tribune* building who refused to take his résumé upstairs. I wasn't as openly hostile to him as the dictator he fled. And I was happy to show him kindness because I enjoyed his stories, admired his perseverance and treasured his loud laugh. But I failed him on a daily basis, quite literally. I wasn't a skilled enough English teacher to help him reach journalistic levels of English fluency.

I cared about Diallo and valued his friendship. Hearing him talk about the war and what it was like to flee in the middle of the night filled me with rage and sorrow on his behalf. Some days, we'd look up from our cups of coffee (black but cut with far more sugar packets than the local Dunkin' Donuts intended for us to take) and stare into each other's eyes, mutually overwhelmed by the tragedy of it all. And on other days, he'd regale me with stories of the articles about which he was most proud or give me advice on my relationship with Kjersti. His kids would tumble into the room and the two of us would lose ourselves in laughter. All that felt real and mutualistic.

But I noticed how I felt knowing that Diallo didn't have this same depth of conversation with *all* the White American staff members, that he didn't invite them to his apartment, that he didn't gift them a traditional Congolese shirt—white but with textured flowers embroidered throughout. I also noticed what I was no longer feeling in those moments: the fear I wasn't doing enough, the fear that teaching refugees to get jobs in hotels was reinforcing rather than disrupting every system I claimed to hate, the nagging feeling that the entire refugee resettlement industry might be a guilt-laundering operation for so many wealthy churches in White-flight suburbs.

Chicago was a way station for Kjersti and me, a centrally located transportation hub that made it easy for her to travel for medical school interviews. After just a year there, we packed up again, this time for the University of Wisconsin School of Medicine and Public Health and a tiny apartment a block off Madison's rowdy frat row. Kjersti was on her way to becoming a family doctor, and desperately needing a job, I signed on as a recruiter for Teach For America.

And then time disappeared in a haze of eighty-hour workweeks and unquestioned ambition. Before I processed what was happening, one year turned into a decade. By 2016, the recruitment gig in Madison had led first into my founding a TFA region in nearby Milwaukee and then to a jet-setting role as the organization's chief marketing officer.

I once recounted that version of my professional story—"I just woke up and suddenly I had a job in the C-suite for a national nonprofit"—to my colleague Teresa, a Black woman who graduated from an elite northeastern liberal arts college. "You know how you sound?" she admonished me. "Like somebody who can just sleepwalk through life, fail upward, and then complain about how his life doesn't have meaning and purpose."

It was the first time I had heard that critique, but it would not be the last. I feared that I caught the eye of higher-ups at TFA only because that organization, like most American organizations, valued the specific brand of charisma that our country cultivates and encourages in its White men. The doubts—about whether I was part of the problem, about whether I had already disappeared into indistinguishable Whiteness, about every choice I had made up to that point—were now at a fever pitch.

At every previous step in my career, I told myself that, because of my relatively humble status in organizational hierarchies, I was still the same young rage-against-the-machine radical who dodged tear gas and lined up for plates of rice and beans served by liberty-spiked Food Not Bombs punks at antiglobalization protests. The problem was, I was no longer an entry-level teacher explaining to my college friends that I joined TFA because "at least it wasn't grad school." I was now a BlackBerry-toting, Delta SkyMiles Medallion–earning, navy-blue-J.Crew-suit-wearing official mouthpiece for a two-thousand-employee organization whose board included several Walmart heirs, a former U.S. Treasury secretary, and multiple *Wall Street Journal*–famous CEOs.

My weeks were a blur of cabs between midtown Manhattan offices and the B Terminal of LaGuardia Airport, of long days spent in cramped conference rooms talking about "returns on investment," "boiling the frog," and "level five leadership" followed by solitary 11:00 p.m. burrito bowls procured from the closest Chipotle, email notifications whirring from the laptop perched on my belly.

One day in 2012, I visited my wife's family in Philadelphia, and my brother-in-law overheard me on the phone with a colleague.

"If you have to talk like that all day," he said when I hung up, "how do you live with yourself?"

I blubbered a response about how he didn't understand the importance of our work, but the words stung.

That same fall, Kjersti and I attended a wedding in Providence, Rhode Island, for one of her college housemates. We shared a room with our mutual friend John—one of the many kids at Earlham who had grown up in a commune and a frequent protest partner back in the day—and his girlfriend, Maria. This was my first time meeting Maria, and she was exactly the kind of never-sold-out radical I wanted to impress. Not only was she a full-time union organizer, but she came from a long line of Salvadorean women who were active in that country's freedom struggles. John and Maria came into our anodyne Providence hotel room with messenger bags and laptops covered with radical stickers, dispatches from the kind of life I didn't choose.

Maria was a foot shorter than me. We hugged politely, exchanged the perfunctory "so good to finally meet you," and then she looked me dead in the eye.

"So, you're, like, a big shot with TFA, huh? You're the enemy."

———

That winter, on a flight home from LaGuardia, I closed my laptop and loaded up a song on my iPod by Tarkio, the jangly folk-country band from Missoula led by a sideburned University of Montana English major named Colin Meloy.

My high school friends and I loved Tarkio. We hung out at Bernice's Bakery, where Meloy bused tables, convinced that he considered the crowd of gawking teenagers to be cool, knowing fellow travelers. My friend Jamie and I schemed to sneak into the band's shows at twenty-one-and-over bars like Jay's or the Union Club, before chickening out at the last minute. It didn't matter that we ended up eating cheese fries at Perkins or Finnegan's; the *idea* of it all was the point.

Jamie went to an all-girls Catholic college in Minnesota. The fall of our respective freshman years, she sent me pictures of herself posing with individual signs spelling out our favorite Tarkio lyric, a line about Albert Camus and how you shouldn't let the bastards get you down. I hung them up all over my room. Friends would come over and ask about them.

"It's hard to explain," I told them. "You have to be from Missoula."

For the duration of the three-minute, banjo-filled song, I felt like the teenager who dreamed of staring down the bastards of the world, not the coffee-guzzling business traveler who was afraid that maybe *he* was the bastard.

I was homesick again. But I wasn't ready to interrogate that homesickness or what it meant for what side I had taken in the religion of being in love/religion of being right dichotomy. Instead, I thought about what consumer purchase could bring back that momentary peace I felt listening to my favorite band from high school. Colin Meloy had, by this point, gone on to a fair bit of national acclaim with his new band, the Portland-based Decemberists. Perhaps I'd feel better if I bought their new album on vinyl. Or, better yet, tickets to their upcoming tour. Maybe that would do the trick.

By the time the plane landed, the moment of potential recognition had passed. I took a cab home to a dark, empty house—Kjersti was working overnight at Saint Luke's on the south side—and collapsed in the same pose as the night before in a midtown Manhattan hotel room.

Fortuitously, in TFA, as was the case in so many non-profits in the 2010s, there was a whole new set of venues in which I could distinguish myself from the morass of Whiteness around me. The diversity-training circles of my college years had, by that decade, become ubiquitous in white-collar workplaces. And while my goal, when I first sat in that earnest, bighearted circle in Earlham's meetinghouse, had once been to mirror what my peers were saying, this was the time for standing out.

These trainings—now called diversity, equity, and inclusion (DEI)—were ostensibly about learning, rather than about anybody's work performance. The fact that our workplace offered them, however, meant that they must be related to *somebody's* work performance. We weren't just learning for learning's sake.

In one of the dozens of DEI sessions that I attended in those disorienting, sleepless TFA-ladder-climbing days, a facilitator proclaimed that this would be a "difficult" session and that we should "get comfortable with being uncomfortable." That phrase struck me as odd. What was uncomfortable about these spaces? They had rules, which meant that I could learn and master those rules. I could get the highest grade possible and finally establish myself as the Valedictorian of Whiteness. I knew I wasn't supposed to be silent when it came time to talk, but I wasn't supposed to talk first either. When I did talk, it was to affirm all the correct answers I already knew coming into the space. Otherwise, I knew to perform a particularly visible form of silent attentiveness: a throwback to my performance in those college-era trainings. Once again, I nodded hard. I pursed my lips. I sighed, but not too loudly and not too frequently.

So many of my White male colleagues were not as well-versed in how to navigate these trainings successfully. I'd listen judgmentally as they'd offer a defensive curriculum vitae of their interracial relationships, their regular contact with the Mexican American kids they used to teach, how they'd never dream of touching a Black woman's hair.

I took note of their mistakes, making a mental list of what not to do.

The sessions usually blurred together. There was little that distinguished a 2011 session from a 2012 session from a 2013 session.

I do remember Denver, though. We spent the whole week in a particularly purgatorial basement conference room. There were no windows. No art on the walls. Just multiple days sitting at white-tableclothed tables and staring at the gray temporary divider walls that delineate space in American hotel ballrooms.

It had been a contentious, exhausting training. The all-White breakout spaces in particular had been argumentative, defensive, and blustery, not unlike the day Loyola Sacred

Heart's senior class attempted to discuss Columbine. By the time we came together for our final session, everybody was spent. Ties were loosened. A growing crowd paced the back of the room, a shared attempt to avoid nodding off in our seats. Our facilitators asked if anybody wanted to make a final statement. A sea of White hands went up.

They haven't learned, I said to myself, *we aren't supposed to get the last word.*

One of the White filibusters was delivered by a guy who was normally gregarious but had been noticeably less so over the course of the session. The entire room broke out of its stupor when he spoke.

"What you all don't know is that I have been listening in on this week's conversation, not as myself, but as a spy. I haven't been a White guy. I've been a Black woman, the mother of one of our students . . . and here's what I think about the ways you were all talking."

And he just kept going.

As a Black mother, he was ashamed of us for not talking more about his children and their potential. We weren't being urgent enough. We didn't understand the stakes for him and his fellow Black mothers. "Our babies can't afford for you all to get this wrong."

I stifled laughter. I wasn't the only one. Others just stared, bug-eyed. And then the facilitators, as tired as the rest of us, closed the session.

Later that evening, I made sure to find a Black colleague with whom I shared a particularly friendly relationship. I noticed Amayah looked upset. Assuming she wanted to talk about what had just happened in the session, I walked up to her and broached the subject.

"Oh man, can you believe that guy?"

"Yeah, pretty crazy."

"Whiteness is a hell of a drug, isn't it? I'm just sorry that you had to hear that. Wow, right? And after how wild so many White people were throughout the whole session. To think that you all were sitting in the session, and he assumed that what we needed to hear was not your actual perspective as a Black woman but him, like, trying to guess how a Black woman might think."

"For sure, it was . . . a lot."

"I mean, that must have felt so insulting."

"You know, it is what it is. I mean, that was just funny. I think, more broadly, it's just so exhausting, the whole non-profit thing. It hurts you more because you get your hopes up that it'll be different. Like, my fiancé works for a bank, so he knows it's gonna just be so White. Like, there's no hope. But here, it sucks, you know, because you get your hopes up."

She started tearing up. In the moment, I processed that Amayah wasn't interested in talking trash about our colleague. I comforted her. But later that night, what lingered was the now-familiar reassurance—never spoken out loud, even to myself, but recognized: if she felt safe enough to tell me, I did something right.

Chapter SIXTEEN

In May 2013, Kjersti gave birth to our first child. We named him for Olof Palme, a former Swedish prime minister. Palme was a committed socialist and a thorn in the sides of the U.S. and apartheid South African governments. He was radical, at least compared with those in the professional circles in which I now found myself.

There were a few reasons for the choice: Kjersti wanted a Swedish name, and there were a number of beautiful, tender details in Palme's biography that we looked forward to passing on to our son. But I know that some of my advocacy for that name had another motive. I was naming my son after somebody who was committed to his values, who never sold out. The name was a challenge I issued to myself.

One of Palme's greatest domestic accomplishments as prime minister was the Miljonprogrammet (Million Program), an ambitious effort to dramatically increase the number of simple, decent affordable homes and apartments available across Sweden. More recently, the legacy of that project has become more complicated. As in many other White majority countries, once immigrants moved into some of the new suburbs created by the project, White Swedes moved out, creating a pattern of government and private sector disinvestment and disrepair. But when it began, the project was a marvel.

I first fell in love with Palme when I found out that he moved his family out of the prime minister's mansion and into one of the modest single-family homes in a Million Program community, a tidy development in a purpose-built Stockholm suburb. There was a photo shoot shortly after the move. In those pictures, he and his wife, Lisbeth, are smiling seraphically as his children play in their tiny backyard. He looks for all the world like a young version of my father. He looks so happy.

As for our Olof, a few months after his birth, the Walt Disney Company released a blockbuster hit movie featuring a dimwitted but lovable snowman sidekick named . . . Olaf. Most people were polite enough to not ask directly if we named our child after a cartoon, but it was still an early lesson in the limits of best laid plans in parenting.

Olof was a terrible sleeper, and I was frequently up with him late at night, which in 2013 meant that I wasn't just thinking terrifying thoughts about whether I had what it took to be his parent, but also that I was on my phone. After all other methods failed, I rocked him to sleep in his car seat, clicking one app after another, cycling through the same emotions every night. I'd read an email and get stressed out about work. I'd scan through one social media app and feel guilty that an old friend had a baby and I hadn't sent a card. I'd click on another and be extremely angry about a stranger's extremely terrible opinions. Most of all, though, I read the news.

Between June and July of 2013, I followed the trial of George Zimmerman, the self-appointed neighborhood vigilante who shot and killed Trayvon Martin, a seventeen-year-old Black Miamian who was visiting his father in Sanford, Florida. Zimmerman became my personal sin-eater as I followed the details of that trial. My anger at him was proof of how well I had metabolized a lifetime of racial justice lessons.

Until a couple of weeks into the trial, I hadn't processed that George Zimmerman wasn't White. Though he could pass for White in the pictures and videos I saw from the courtroom, his mother was Afro-Peruvian, and Zimmerman self-identified as Hispanic. Still, it was easier for me to think of him as fully White. It made the story cleaner. White people, particularly White people who weren't me, were the problem.

On July 13, 2013, around 9:00 p.m. central time, the verdict was announced. Olof was, somewhat remarkably, asleep. I waited outside his room in anticipation of soon needing to walk him. My most distinct memory of that evening was the phantom limb sensation of my son *not* being on my chest. That's what I noticed when Zimmerman's acquittal was announced. *My son isn't here, but he will be tomorrow morning. Trayvon won't.* My heart dropped. An honest, empathetic human reaction.

There is a version of this story where I felt no need to publicly insert my reaction into the story. There's a version where I simply felt sad, debriefed with Kjersti, and went to bed. There's a version where I woke up the next morning, hugged my son, and then reflected on how I might become a better partner for racial justice. None of those is the path I took.

"Thinking about Trayvon's mom and dad," I wrote on Facebook, "and a nation of parents of black boys who are forced to question again tonight about whether our country loves and holds their children in our arms."

My modest and honest post received a tidy collection of algorithmically aided likes and a few messages from Black friends, colleagues, and acquaintances to the effect of "thanks for saying something."

I went to bed still grieving the verdict, but no longer exclusively. I noticed the responses. I clocked the affirmations. In moments such as this, I now knew what to do.

Chapter SEVENTEEN

I turned thirty-five in the spring of 2016. At the time, I was still working for TFA. A year and a half earlier, my previous role as head of the Milwaukee region opened again, and I asked if I could leave my national position and return to focusing on the region. It was a pragmatic decision. I had a baby at home. Being out on the road was both logistically unsustainable and spiritually devastating.

Even though I wasn't coming back *for* the role, I threw myself into it with a renewed energy. This was my chance to show how different I was thanks to all that solemn nodding in all those trainings. Our Milwaukee team was going to be the most diverse, equitable, and inclusive workplace in our city. We would be a true beloved community, laughing together, challenging one another, pushing each other to "ground ourselves in the neighborhoods where we work" and "decolonize our language" and "speak truth to power."

Of all the places where I could prove myself to be the

world's most liberatory White male boss, doing so in Milwaukee mattered. Like Doland, Milwaukee was once a city of idealistic dreamers. An outsized percentage of the Germans who streamed into town in the 1800s and 1900s were abolitionists and socialists. Not far from my house, on a hill with a panoramic view of downtown, was the intersection of Booth Street and Glover Avenue. Joshua Glover was an enslaved Black man who, in 1852, escaped from Missouri before being captured and temporarily jailed in Milwaukee in 1854. Sherman Booth was an antislavery newspaper editor who, in March of that year, led a mob of White Milwaukeeans to storm the jail, freeing Glover, who then fled to Canada. The story of Booth and Glover evoked a time when White Milwaukee still believed it had escaped culpability for America's original sin.

Milwaukee didn't tell stories like that about itself anymore. It was a Rust Belt town that had followed the same patterns as other once-prosperous industrial meccas. For more than a century, there were plentiful jobs in southeast Wisconsin to support wave after wave of White ethnic migrants. These new Milwaukeeans were permitted to live anywhere and send their kids to any school they pleased. There were also jobs for Black migrants from the South and Latinos from Mexico and Puerto Rico, though those Milwaukeeans were never granted the same civic privileges afforded to the Germans, Irish, Poles, and Slavs.

When the jobs were plentiful, White Milwaukeeans lived in the city and flocked to Serb Hall on the south side for political speeches by old-school liberal Democrats—Hubert Humphrey and the Kennedy brothers. As the jobs dried up, those same White people followed the new interstates to the suburbs. The angriest among them hurled bricks and bottles at civil rights marchers. The more polite continued to flock to Serb Hall, this time for speeches not by Humphrey but by the infamous segregationist governor of Alabama, George Wallace, who proudly proclaimed that if he were not a proud son of Dixie, he would wish he was born on the south side of Milwaukee.

If I could be a truly great White male boss here—in a city now considered one of the most segregated in the country—that would really prove something. If my team was diverse and equitable and we all loved each other, if Black and Brown community leaders looked at us and marveled at our thoughtfulness and inclusion, if we could claim to be a "model of anti-racism," then perhaps all my doubts would finally disappear for good.

A couple of days before my birthday, my colleagues and I went out to a bar together to celebrate. We did not do so fully voluntarily, mind you. When I took over the executive director role, I decreed that when anybody had a birthday, they picked a group social event that we all did together.

I made a fair number of mandates like that one. I was the kind of boss who loved to talk about "workplace culture" and "belonging." We had hip, matching crewneck sweatshirts—clean sans serif white font on black. They looked like Brooklyn Nets jerseys. They were sharp, cohesive, just like the team

I had built. I was excited all week for the night out. It was one more chance to show that we were more than just colleagues. I told Kjersti I'd be back late.

I arrived at Camino and immediately spotted a few co-workers huddled at a couple of tables near the front windows: Tom, Sarah, and Maria, our office's extroverts, the crew I expected to show up first. Sarah ordered some pierogi and cheese curds for the table—the latter were Camino's specialty; the former were a happy hour freebie. I took a couple sips of my beer and directed my attention to the appetizers. The curds were as advertised. They were made just down the street, this being a neighborhood that used to be full of tanneries and then was full of empty tanneries and was just starting to be filled with artisan cheesemakers. The paint on the bike lanes was still fresh; the potholes I maneuvered around to get here felt like they'd been there forever.

But, oh God, the cheese curds were so good: discernibly sharp cheddar, molten without being scalding. I forgave the unnecessarily cheffy jalapeño berry dipping sauce taking up space in a ramekin that should have been filled with ranch dressing.

We plowed our way through the cheese curds almost as soon as they hit the table. I tried not to eat too many, tried not to be noticed taking too many, tried, of course, not to take the last one.

It didn't take long for my other colleagues to show up. There were about fifteen of us—enough to more than fill the couple of tables by the window. A few folks established a satellite location toward the cramped, narrow back end of the bar. I made the rounds.

As a group, we stood out. We were diverse in that perfectly curated college admissions brochure way. Our team included a couple of Black colleagues, Jada and William, who had grown up in Black neighborhoods here in Milwaukee. Our donors often asked them to tell stories about challenges they had overcome in "those neighborhoods." There was another Black colleague, Michelle, who grew up in Mequon, a tony outer ring suburb whose schools are often breathlessly described as the best in the state. She, in turn, was expected to tell stories about how grateful she was to have been raised in such a good community. There was Maria, who was Puerto Rican and whose grandma worked in our office building when it was an actual tannery, as well as Iqra, who was Palestinian and had attended high school down the street, in a new building that looked for all the world like a prison crossed with a mall. Iqra, whose name I long thought I was pronouncing correctly but I never quite got right, was the first colleague to tell me when I was being a typical bro-ey White guy boss: talking over female colleagues, overpraising charismatic men, making sure I got my way on decisions large and small. At that point, I truly believed that I had heard, internalized, and overcome that feedback.

We were from Milwaukee, Chicagoland, the Quad Cities, Hawaii, St. Louis, and various towns in Wisconsin. We were White and Mexican and Peruvian and Vietnamese and Japanese. We were gay and straight, all fairly young. A true post-Obama dream team. United Colors of Nonprofit Exceptionalism.

Our office was just up the street in a stately Cream City brick colossus. At one point, 50 percent of all the leather in the city of Milwaukee was produced in and around our building—first by the Germans, then by the Slavs and Poles, and finally by the Puerto Ricans and Mexicans. The whole thing finally shut down around 2000. I didn't know anything about tanning leather. None of us did. We all worked at computers. We wrote grant reports. We used terms like "youth empowerment" and "stakeholder engagement" and "breaking the cycle of poverty and segregation."

I checked in with all our tables. The conversation seemed to be flowing along just fine. Nothing memorable was said, but everybody got along—just a quiet hum of pleasantries from people who didn't really have anything new to report. I shot a few glances at the *Burger Time* arcade game in the back hallway, hoping that somebody might ask if I was up for a game. There was no reason for them to know that, back when I lived in Clancy, I snuck into my older brothers' room to play their *Burger Time* handheld game.

Before long, a couple of colleagues returned from a conversation with another group of happy hour-ers with exciting news: our noticeable diversity had, in fact, been noticed. The other group gushed about how nice it was to see a group "like us" out together in a city like Milwaukee: "You don't see that around town enough—good for you." My colleagues seemed pleased by the compliment. I tried to play it cool, but I was ecstatic. We all clinked glasses.

Still glowing from the strangers' affirmation, it took me a moment to realize that the conversation had abruptly turned toward goodbyes. I sipped my beer slower, sending a subconscious signal that we could all relax and keep hanging out. But one by one, my colleagues called it a night. It was still light out.

Around the second departure, a full, weighty chill came over my body. Had I been fifteen years old in a Methodist church somewhere in Montana, I might have assumed that God was speaking to me. Now I knew the opposite was true. The chill meant that I was alone, and I knew precisely why I was alone.

I tried not to show my emotional cards, but I failed. Jada, a teacher coach who was particularly skilled at seeing below the surface of a situation, looked up from her beer and stared at me, her eyes concerned and probing.

"Garrett, what's going on?"

I answered honestly: "I'm really sad."

"Why?"

That was too much honesty. I tried to dial it back. "Um, well, it's hard to explain."

"No seriously, why?"

I couldn't admit that I'd had grand dreams for what that night could have been. I couldn't admit that I was this shaken by something as banal as my colleagues wanting to leave a work-mandated happy hour early. I couldn't admit that it was that simple.

"You know, I don't know what it is. I must just be feeling weird about my birthday."

A few days later, when Jada brought up that moment again, I claimed that the main reason I said anything at all was to make it easier for folks like her to feel safe sharing their feelings. Further proof that I was running out of rope.

In that moment at Camino, though, my mumbled nonanswer did the trick. Thoroughly embarrassed, I now wanted to be alone. I got my wish. Not long after I admitted I felt sad, Jada and the last two stragglers left. I hurriedly finished the remainder of my beer and headed back to the bar to pay my tab. I mumbled to the bartender that I shouldn't have left a tab open. He stared blankly back at me, unmoved by my superflous clarification.

I followed my colleagues' lead and left the bar, avoiding eye contact with the table of people who, just a few minutes prior, had been successfully fooled into thinking that this was anything more than what it was: a group of colleagues asked to take an additional hour out of their Friday by the person who signed their paychecks. I walked outside, got into my car, and cried.

Chapter EIGHTEEN

The morning after I cried in my car, I woke up and went back to work. The busier I made myself, the less I thought about why something as silly as a shortened, lonely happy hour left me so devastated. I delivered workshops for our teachers, pitched to donors, and then came home and took care of Olof. I kept moving.

I also dug further into my bag of tricks. I spent the summer of 2016 waiting for tragedy and then, when it presented itself, writing about it online. That was the original summer of viral videos of cops killing Black men: Alton Sterling in Louisiana. Philando Castile outside of St. Paul.

They were horrific videos, self-evidently so, but that didn't stop me from repeating the fact of their terribleness in piece after piece. Those essays, in turn, were read and shared by other people who wanted help processing the deaths they had just witnessed. My brain was in laboratory rat mode. I pressed a button and got a reward. I wrote an essay and watched it get passed around on Facebook with captions like "THIS" or

"Garrett does it again" or, the best, "White people, this is what it looks like to be an ally."

For the first half of that summer, I once again had a purpose. I didn't have to think about my day job. I acted as if the world truly counted on me to write impassioned jeremiads about race. I wasn't doing this for the dopamine. I was doing it because I was an ally to Black people, a race traitor to Whiteness, basically John Brown with an internet connection.

The trick worked well until it didn't.

August 13 was hot. It was one of those *Do the Right Thing* days where kids just hang out in the street and wait for something to happen. It was the kind of day that bleeds into the kind of night where, if a couple of young guys get pulled over and then one of them makes a run for it and then a cop shoots and kills him, a crowd gathers. In this case, the victim's name was Sylville Smith. The cop's name was Dominique Heaggan-Brown. They were both Black and from the same neighborhood, Sherman Park, but Heaggan-Brown had a reputation in the community as a particularly vindictive and mean cop. Word got out. The crowd grew larger and the cops brought out the riot gear and one thing led to another, and by sundown, there were businesses on fire all around the intersection of Burleigh Street and Sherman Boulevard.

I was home that night. Olof was sort of sleeping. Kjersti was at the hospital. I heard—maybe from texts, more likely from the internet—that something was popping off in Sherman Park. I turned on the news and saw the fires and the riot cops, and it looked exactly like recent uprisings in Baltimore,

Baton Rouge, and Ferguson, except this time everything was familiar.

A gas station and a few stores were torched. I recognized all of them. I didn't recognize any of the kids yelling at the cops or staring down the line of tanks, but that felt like a minor detail. I had been writing about police murders and community uprisings all summer, and now one was here.

I checked in with Kjersti to ensure that she had a safe route home. I convinced myself that, once again, others were counting on me to write. I didn't ask myself if that was actually a healthy way to process live images of riot cops staring down crowds of angry, frightened kids. I was just glad that I had something to do. I sat down and started typing, but fell asleep before I could finish my essay.

I woke up the next morning feeling self-conscious. I still wanted to finish the essay, but convinced myself that this time I had to do more. This was my city. I lived here. I needed to take responsibility for it. I didn't want to write a piece and publish it and then have somebody ask me, "What did you do on the ground?" and not have an answer.

I got dressed and asked Kjersti if she could stay with Olof so that I could head over to the center of the melee to help clean up. Before I could even get out the door, though, one of my TFA teachers texted a group of us to say that there was no need to come down—a large crowd had already shown up that morning. I wasn't the only Milwaukeean with the same idea for how to be useful.

At least I tried.

Not knowing what else to do, I opened the office for any teachers who wanted to come in and process the previous evening's events. About a dozen of them did. The group included a couple of our Black teachers who grew up not far from Sherman Park as well as a handful of Black and Latina teachers from other cities who wanted to compare notes on how different or similar Sherman Park was to their own communities. The rest of the teachers who showed up were White; like me, they sought direction. All the teachers who came were women. We hung around for an hour or so, before realizing we didn't have much more to say other than the obvious. We exchanged hugs, and I sent them on their way.

After they left, I wrote.

The essay didn't take long to finish. It was all fairly boilerplate by now, the latest in a series of polemics where I told other White people that whatever they were doing was wrong. The unspoken insinuation was that I, the author of the piece, wasn't making the same mistakes they were. In this case I told them to desegregate Milwaukee by spending less time around White people and more time around Black people. I namechecked specific places and businesses and organizations. I used exclamation points to confer a sense of urgency.

I published the piece and traded texts with friends and colleagues. The consensus was that the next couple of evenings were going to be rough. I had recently read an earnest essay titled "What White People Should Do at Black-Led Protests," which argued that cops were less likely to attack White people, so bodies like mine were useful in deescalating tense situations. That was all the confirmation I needed that my specific presence was necessary that evening. If what it took to finally cleanse my guilt was the corporal infliction of pain, so be it. Sign me up for absolution by cop.

It took fifteen minutes or so to travel the long, straight line west toward Sherman Park. I arrived a bit before dusk. I drove around aimlessly, circling the same four-block radius a few times before fully committing to stopping. Now that I was here, I was nervous. I may have overstated my appetite for physical risk and danger.

With no good excuse to keep stalling, I finally parked and walked around. I had no idea what I was supposed to do. It was cooler than the previous evening, a pleasant night for a walk. If you ignored all the boarded-up businesses on the neighborhood's main commercial drag, Sherman Park was bucolic, full of well-kept bungalows and mature leafy trees.

I cut through the neighborhood's namesake park and walked down West Burleigh Street: a key thoroughfare not just here, but in my neighborhood as well. There was nothing familiar about these blocks, though, nor should there have been. I hadn't walked on this section of West Burleigh Street before.

I texted William, a Black colleague who grew up in the neighborhood: "I'm here!"

He replied that he was here too, but he didn't mention anything about trying to link up.

I walked for less than five minutes and started to distrust that article. Did I really need to be here? Five more minutes passed. The answer, quite clearly, was no. I got back into my car and felt multiple feelings at once. I was both relieved and unsettled. I felt as if I had just walked into a room that I expected to be full, and instead, when I opened the door, the lights were off and the chairs were stacked on the tables and it was unclear whether the problem was that I shouldn't be in the room, that I was late, or that I was early.

I turned on the radio. Sherman Park wasn't even in the news anymore. Somewhere far from Milwaukee, Donald Trump was holding a rally, which meant breathless reports about whether he said something boorish and whether the crowds screamed. Trump was filling arenas that summer, and here I was, thinking I was saving the country because I could write increasingly popular Facebook posts.

Kjersti had told me that I didn't need to rush home that night, so I had time on my hands. Still with no idea what to do with myself, I turned west on Burleigh, in the opposite direction of my house. Before long, Black neighborhoods gave way to White suburbs. The familiar American signifiers that declared a neighborhood is likely to be poor and Black—cracked sidewalks, boarded-up businesses, an absence of any clear social democratic investment—gave way to the signifiers of middle-class Whiteness. The lawns became manicured. The streetlights shined brighter. The stores grew bigger and boxier. I might as well have been back in Columbia, except I wasn't. I was less than twenty minutes from my house, still in Milwaukee County.

At least in theory, this was where those people whom

I addressed in all those online diatribes lived. But here too there was nobody who needed me, nor was there anybody here I needed.

Worn down by the inertia of the night, I stopped by a McDonald's drive-through for a plain vanilla ice cream. The teenager working the window was polite as she told me my total, took my money, and handed me a cake cone filled with soft serve and too few napkins for the mess I would soon make of myself. It was the only direct interaction I had with another human being all night. By the time I got home, Kjersti was asleep. My colleague in Sherman Park never texted me with an update, nor did I expect him to.

PART FIVE

Coming Home

Chapter NINETEEN

W hat is perhaps most incongruous about this entire period of my life, filled as it was with thirsty striving for attention and validation on the professional front, was how all those insecurities largely disappeared when I walked in the back door of my house. That's not to say that life with a three-year-old was rejuvenating or free from doubts. Both Kjersti and I worried, as I imagine all parents do, that somehow either our deficiencies as parents or the brokenness of the world would somehow tamp down what we loved most about our son: his snuggly gentleness, his genuine interest in us ("Mommy, was today a better day at work?"), and his soulful introspection. Olof had a big, raucous laugh, but when I was away from him, the image that was perennially frozen in my mind was always his contemplation face: head tilted to the side, his giant green eyes fixed on an arbitrary spot in the middle distance.

We had all the same fears as other parents, Kjersti and I, but they didn't overwhelm. We knew why. In one of the most serendipitous occurrences in our life, we discovered that not only did we love and respect each other as previously childless peers, but we also had similar orientations toward parenting. We had the same instincts as to when to set a boundary, when to allow an extra dessert, when to play wild tickling and tackling games versus quiet time with books and trains. There were differences, to be sure. I learned daily from Kjersti's appropriate but not overbearing sense of how to keep him physically safe. But in large part, whether we were parenting well or poorly, we weren't racked with daily anxiety because at least we were doing it together.

I loved Kjersti so much before this era, but I came to respect her even more deeply. She became a mom at the same moment that she became a doctor. I knew how she was at home; I knew that we trusted each other with Olof. But it was a delight to go out to the occasional happy hour or brunch or work event and hear her colleagues, including older mentors, talk about how much they learned from her, how innately she cared for and listened to her patients, how fastidious she was in seeking out humanistic solutions to medical dilemmas. For all my performative flailing outside the house, it was a joy to come home and be her partner. Shortly after Olof was born, back when he was breastfeeding, she made a single rule:

"If I feed him, you feed me."

It was a simple charge, and one I was happy to follow. I loved coming home and making dinner and doing the dishes. I loved Sunday grocery shopping with Olof perched in the cart.

Also notable: while I worried for Olof's future, I didn't *need* anything from him. I was grateful for his gentleness *now*. I didn't need him to accomplish anything to earn his worthiness, either as a human being generally or as a White boy specifically. I didn't need him to achieve, to prove anything about his family lineage, to receive the world's acclaim. I just loved him.

I didn't notice the contrast between my feelings as a parent and the narrative I had developed for myself as a son. I still wasn't ready to trust my parents and their lifetime of assurances that, just as it was for me with Olof, so too was it for them with me. I wasn't ready because that narrative was never their creation in the first place. It was my story, and it would remain my story until I was finally ready to replace it with a new one.

I didn't notice this contrast in spite of the fact that my parents were now *here*, in Milwaukee, living just a mile to the east of us. They had grandbabies spread across the country, from Portland, Oregon, to Washington, D.C., so they chose Milwaukee for its relative ease in helping them see the growing next generation of Buckses. It was cheap and had an airport and was as "in the middle" as you could be in this vast country. So they were Milwaukeeans now, right here with us; not asking anything from me, just helping us out and delighting in having at least one of their grandchildren this close.

I couldn't help but feel guilty that they were here, though. It was one more act of immense kindness and intentionality on their part. Yes, I was the Bucks sibling who happened to live in a midwestern city with a large-enough airport and relatively affordable housing for a now retired couple, but they could have decided to live closer to any of their grandchildren, and yet they were here. And for that I felt both immense gratitude and immense guilt.

There was another clear reason that our family life in 2016 was so blessedly pacific. In February, Kjersti learned that she was pregnant with our second child. We hugged and cried, waited nervously for a few weeks, and then hugged and cried again. After Olof, there had been a couple of miscarriages. The first was a particular gut punch. We lost a baby late in the first trimester, not long after we started telling our families.

Kjersti and Olof were at her parents' place when she texted me that she thought the baby was gone. I sped to the airport, booking a last-minute ticket at red lights. When I boarded the tiny Delta commuter plane, Kjersti was on her way to the hospital. By the time I landed in Minneapolis, the news was official. We bawled together on the phone—her outside her parents' house, me frozen on a moving walkway.

I hated the Minneapolis airport that day. The walk from my gate to the shuttle that would take me to the southern Minnesota college town where my in-laws lived, felt like a marathon. Assuming that they couldn't understand what I was going through, I stared at everybody I passed, judging them for not being visibly heartbroken, resenting their vacant stares and obsession with their phones. There was a core irony in that assumption, of course. The source of my heartbreak that day wasn't uncommon. It was one of the more universal experiences faced by couples. Had I sat down at an airport bar and explained how my day was going to five people, odds are that at least one of them would have had their own story to tell. But that's not how I felt in that moment. I felt alone in a major international airport, and until I could finally embrace Kjersti, I wanted to wallow in that aloneness.

We were happy that February, but nervous. But with each successive month, a bit more of that anxiety was replaced with anticipatory joy. At work, I was a mess. Out in the world, I kept screaming, *See me! Affirm me! Tell me I'm doing this right!* But at home, I was grateful. We were lucky, Kjersti and I. We got a chance to do this together, again.

We finally felt confident telling Olof early in the summer. He was obsessed with trains, so my mother, ever intentional, bought a Woody Guthrie–inspired picture book called *New Baby Train* for the occasion.

Chapter TWENTY

Three days after Sherman Park burned, Donald Trump came to West Bend, Wisconsin. Although I paid a great deal of attention to Trump rallies in those days, cringing at lines that I decided offended my liberal sensibilities, I never watched a whole event.

That summer, a popular feedback loop had emerged, where media outlets conducted emotionally generous profiles of Trump voters (the most infamous were sit-downs in various Rust Belt diners), and the kind of people I wanted to impress (left-leaning people of color with large internet followings) expressed their outrage that people who were attracted to Trump's incendiary rhetoric would receive such fawning treatment. I got the message: for the sake of my progressive bona fides, I would not show any sympathy or curiosity for Trump voters. If they wanted me to care about them as people, they could have the good sense to agree with me.

I made the time for the West Bend rally, though. I knew

West Bend well. It was a forty-five-minute shot northwest from my house. Like the city where I lived, it was settled by Germans and bisected by the same placid Milwaukee River. I'd heard it called a Milwaukee exurb, but that was a bit of a stretch. It was one of many mostly White satellites distantly circling the big, mostly Black and Brown city.

I knew West Bend because Kjersti's grandpa lived there, in an expansive senior citizens home on the edge of town. For me, West Bend was a U-shaped complex full of elderly White people, a city within a city of five o'clock suppers, model train rooms, and wide hallways to accommodate motorized wheelchairs. I knew that Grandpa Howie wasn't going to the Trump rally, but I had a hunch that some of his neighbors, men and women who doted on Olof when we visited, would be there.

There were so many things about my own Whiteness that I now questioned, but Donald Trump as a signifier of everything I rejected wasn't one of them. He fetishized wealth. He was cruel and mocking. He said all the things I knew not to say.

Truth be told, I loved having Trump traveling around the country doing Trump-y things that summer. He was a never-ending fuel source for liberal consternation. I could walk into meetings with other upper-middle-class nonprofit professionals, and none of us would have to admit that we were deeply unsure whether our life's work was helping or hurting our "partner communities." We could say, "Did you hear what he said about the wall? Or how he mocked that disabled reporter? Or the way he told his crowd to rough up the protesters?" "It's so scary," we'd all agree. "And those crowds, like, who are those people?"

I told myself that I needed to watch the West Bend rally, however, in order to be on the lookout for clear and present danger. I needed to see, in real time, what he said about Milwaukee, Black Milwaukee in particular. But I really watched because this time I *was*, in fact, curious about the crowd. These weren't my neighbors, but they could be. They could include the kindly elderly people who lived with Kjersti's grandpa.

I knew, or I presumed I knew, how Howie's neighbors voted. Washington County made up one-third of what political scientists called the "WOW counties" (Ozaukee and Waukesha were the other two). Together, they formed a collar around Milwaukee County that, throughout the 2000s, was known as being among the most dependable Republican strongholds in the entire nation. We did not talk politics during our visits to Howie's apartment.

The rally wasn't what I expected. It wasn't held in an arena or an aircraft hangar, but the comparatively cozy confines of the Washington County fairgrounds. About two thousand folks squeezed inside, though Trump assured his audience that plenty more were outside. The event was clearly designed by Trump's team as more of an address than one of his famously loose call-and-response spectacles. The fans in attendance did their best to whoop, yell, and boo at the proper moments, but, at least for the first hour of the rally, they didn't get to do any of that summer's big MAGA arena rock hits. No *"Build the wall!"* or *"Lock her up!"* Just a few "Trump, Trump, Trumps" and "U.S.A., U.S.A.s."

With at least some of the now familiar Trump-y theatrics stripped away, what I was left with was the most fascinating political speech I had ever heard. The West Bend address, deliberately timed as a response to the Sherman Park uprising, was clearly intended as the Trump campaign's grand pitch to Black voters in big cities. Trump repeatedly spoke about being "here in Milwaukee," which, coming immediately after nationally televised images of Black Milwaukee kids facing off against riot cops, inferred that he was talking to Black people. But every time there was an applause break after a "here in Milwaukee" line, the crowd's response was tepid. Any southeast Wisconsinite could have told Trump that would be the case. A White crowd in West Bend wouldn't think of themselves as being "from Milwaukee" in 2016, just as a Black or Brown Milwaukeean would never claim to be from West Bend.

But that wasn't the most obvious tell. The real giveaway was the pronouns. Black people were evoked regularly throughout the speech, but always as in the third person.

"Our job is not to make life more comfortable for the rioter or the robber or the looter or the violent disrupter, of which there are many. Our job is to make life more comfortable for the African American parent who wants their kids to be able to safely—safely—walk the streets and walk to school . . .

"We reject the bigotry of Hillary Clinton, which panders to and talks down to communities of color and sees them only as votes, that's all they care about, not as individual human beings worthy of a better future. They have taken advantage . . .

"I understand that a lot of powerful people are in our

political system. A lot of people who've created our problems will lose a lot of their contracts and a lot of their money if African American voters and all the minority voters support my campaign. That I know, that I know for sure."

As his speech carried on, my detached smugness faded. This was much more familiar than I wanted it to be. It's not that I agreed with any of it. It's that I was counting on Trump's rhetoric to not only be detestable but to be completely unlike anything I might say. I expected the kids out in Sherman Park to be derided as thugs, for Blackness to be pathologized, for "culture" or "fatherlessness" to be blamed, for his audience to leave with the assurance that their Whiteness was guiltless because somebody else's Blackness was guilty.

But that's not what Trump was doing here. I could still critique this address if I wanted to feel better about myself. I could write a snarky Facebook post and tell my nonprofit-employed friends that I watched a whole Trump speech where he pretended that he was in Milwaukee when he actually wasn't, or about how he kept talking about Black people as if they were an alien species. And I did a bit of that the next day, but it was half-hearted, more muscle memory than conviction.

The problem was, just two days previously, I drove to Sherman Park pretending that the residents of that neighborhood and I were a shared "we" and ended up eating a fast-food ice-cream cone alone in my car. At least Trump was honest in his choice of pronouns. As far as Black Milwaukee was concerned, he and I were both "theys," both of us trying to prove that we were the allies to communities to which we had no real relationship whatsoever.

Later that night, I saw a ghost. A newspaper out of Madison posted one of those videos where a journalist interviewed those in line to watch Trump's speech to find out what about the Make America Great Again message appealed to them. I don't remember any of the attendees' answers, but I remember seeing him. He wasn't being interviewed, so I know nothing about him, least of all why he supported Trump. He was just in the background. Face full of crags and crevices. Compact frame giving way to a late-in-life paunch. Glasses chosen for utility rather than style. Crisp, striped short-sleeved button-down work shirt. A single breast pocket, stuffed with a yellow farmer's notebook and a clickable pen. A green cap.

He looked like so many other midwestern White men of a certain age. He was clearly either a farmer or somebody whose livelihood depended on farmers. His arms were crossed, his expression taciturn. I couldn't stop staring at him, which is to say that I couldn't stop staring at the ghost of my grandfathers. George Gelston and Russell Bucks were not identical-looking men, but somehow, he looked like both of them. That deep canyon of a face. The tired eyes, the kind that looked like they had just finished staring at an unpaid bill. The downturned mouth that you just know could erupt in a wide-eyed smile if a child jumped in his lap. I had seen that face before.

There they were, both my grandfathers, raised from the dead and plopped down in Washington County, Wisconsin. Waiting in line at a Trump rally, staring back at me through the screen, denying me the relief of an explanation for why they were there or what it meant.

The ghost's hat was green, with the familiar blossom-rising-from-infinity-loop logo of the Pioneer Hi-Bred International seed company. Pioneer. That's what we were, for better or worse, us Buckses and Gelstons: pioneers. There was a story to that hat and to the company it represented. Pioneer Hi-Bred was founded by Henry Wallace, the onetime pride of Orient, Iowa. He was FDR's secretary of agriculture and vice president, a race radical, a friend to workers and farmers, a mentor to Hubert Humphrey, and a hero in towns like Doland. His fall from grace was both complicated and simple: he wouldn't condemn the USSR, so he was pushed out of the administration. Harry Truman took his place, first as vice president and then, when FDR died, as president.

I used to believe that if Henry Wallace had become president, everything would have been different. Slowly but surely, I was letting go of that great man story. But now this ghost of both of my grandfathers was staring at me, wearing *that* hat, reminding me that whatever was happening here, I was connected to it. I couldn't run from it. By the end of the rally, the crowd finally got to chant, *"Build that wall!"* And I had tried. Lord knows I had tried. I'd been building that wall for years—between me and them. The problem was, it wasn't holding.

Chapter TWENTY-ONE

O n Election Day 2016, Kjersti was thirty-eight weeks pregnant. She woke up that morning with a strong premonition that the baby would be born before the end of the night. We both considered her instincts on this matter to be pretty damn ironclad; within twenty-four hours of her getting that exact same premonition during her first pregnancy, we cradled Olof for the first time.

That morning, we all took a family trip to our polling place, the bilingual public elementary school that both kids would eventually attend, and posed for pictures with our I VOTED stickers. We put one on Olof's light fall jacket and then let him place one on his mother's pregnant belly. We imagined this as the day where we'd vote together in the morning and become a family of four before nightfall. We didn't know if the new baby was a boy or girl, but Kjersti had her premonitions on that front as well. Kjersti and I were both to the left of Hillary Clinton, but we were still eager to connect our family story to a historical moment. Our daughter, born on the day the United States elected its first woman president. What a story.

The thing about surprises is that they leave no time for rehearsed, curated reactions. Whichever way your body and brain instinctually conspire to react at the moment of a discovery is, in fact, your honest reaction. So yes, I was surprised the night that Trump was elected. I recoiled instinctually. I didn't see it coming.

As soon as the official call was made late that Tuesday night, my phone was filled with "This can't be happening" and "I'm moving to Canada" texts from other city-dwelling, college-educated White liberal friends. I logged on to Facebook, which was flooded with tear-filled post after tear-filled post. I wanted to believe that somehow I was processing this moment differently from others in my cohort, but I wasn't. In the moment when the election was called, my brain and body responded in the same way as those of virtually every other college-educated White liberal. I *was* shocked. I *couldn't* believe that this was happening. I *would have loved* to move to Canada.

Kjersti fell asleep before the results were announced. When she read the news the morning of November 9, she too had an instant brain-body response. She stood in front of me, tears streaming down her face.

"I don't think the baby is ready to come yet."

My daughter wasn't born on Election Day. Nor was she born the next day. There was no rational reason to panic, but I wasn't feeling especially rational. Kjersti was only at thirty-eight weeks. There was no hard-and-fast rule that our baby's birth *had* to correspond with a major national political event. But that's how it felt. A nation of Trump voters was messing with our baby.

In every direction I turned, I found another White person with my same demographic signifiers having exactly the same reaction. No matter which tactic I tried, another White liberal had already gotten there first. These were the days when some White people started wearing safety pins on their clothing (to supposedly denote to an immigrant that they were a safe person who did not wish to immediately deport them). These were also the days when other White people immediately lobbied self-righteous critiques against the safety pin wearers.

I did both, in quick succession. I put on a safety pin, promptly removed it, then silently derided anybody I saw still wearing theirs.

One of my national TFA colleagues at the time, Harriet, was, in addition to her day job, a well-known Black Lives Matter activist with a sizable social media following. Ours was the kind of relationship that I described as a "close friendship" but that she likely described as "collegial." We were on text terms, but usually only when I initiated.

Shortly after Kjersti told me that our baby was not ready to enter the world, I noticed that one of Harriet's tweets went viral. Watching the likes and retweets pile up under her missive—something to the effect of "White people, this is your problem, what's your plan?"—I wanted her to know that, unlike other White people, I *was* developing a plan.

"Hey," I texted. "I think I might actually have an idea—there's something I'd like to put together organizing White people."

Harriet's reply was speedy and polite: "You should talk to Jason."

I knew Jason. He was another White guy who worked for an education nonprofit and wrote a lot of social media posts about how White people needed to "do better."

At first I read Harriet's text as an affirmation. It was only a few days later that I realized she was likely fielding hundreds of White people texts just as sweaty as mine, all of us seeking the affirmation of the one prominent Black activist whose number was saved in our phone.

I did reach out to Jason, but both of us balked when it came time to move from "we should talk" to *actually* talking. It's not that I lied when I told Harriet that I had a potential plan. I really had been thinking about doing some variety of organizing with other White people. It was only a glimmer of an idea, but ever since I saw that ghost in the Pioneer hat, I wondered what it might look like to turn toward other White people rather than away.

But that didn't mean I was fully ready to *actually talk* to another White person about my idea. That would mean collaboration. That would make me that much less visionary. I bet that I would have benefited a lot from brainstorming with Jason, but it was easier to let inertia take the wheel.

I spent those weeks worrying about our baby and thinking about other White people. The green-hatted ghost. The armies of flailing, Trump-sick college-educated liberals, all of them having the same reaction as me. Trump himself, so nakedly ambitious, so clearly trying to fill a hole in his heart through other people's affirmations, so much more like me than I wanted to admit.

On November 22, a couple weeks after the election, our daughter, Ida Jane, was finally born. We pronounced her name the Swedish way, with a hard *e*, but were also pleased that it tied her both to Ida B. Wells and to her maternal great-grandmother. The Jane part was for my mother.

For the next few months, I was gifted with the most basic, existential tether to the love side of the being in love vs. being right theological divide. I had a newborn to cuddle and stare at and imagine, in her face, a universe of belonging and connection. She had the same world-enveloping eyes as her brother and mother. Even as a baby, we could already see glimpses of the girl she would grow into—brave, curious, hilarious. My goodness was she a delight. Once again, I didn't doubt anything within the four walls of our house. But as was the case with her brother, I walked her to sleep with a phone in my hand.

Chapter TWENTY-TWO

In the spring of 2017, I officially quit my job with TFA. I called myself a consultant now, following a storied tradition of white-collar professionals who want to buy themselves more time before figuring out what to do with their lives. Most of my clients were TFA regions. For all my angst and critiques while working for TFA, the organization was always kinder and more generous toward me than I was toward it.

My primary reason for leaving was to spend more time not merely saying that I had a plan to work with other White people but actually developing that plan.

One weekend in April, Kjersti's parents came down to help her watch the kids, and I decamped for a railroad car turned vacation rental on a farm outside Decorah, Iowa. My goal was to make sense of everything that had been rattling around my head since that West Bend rally.

I called my idea The Barnraisers Project. My dream was to train White organizers from across the country to mobilize their own communities for racial justice. I had a vision for what that might look like both in the Columbias and Missoulas of the world as well as the Clancys and Dolands. I wrote nonstop that weekend, the ideas just falling out of me.

Technically, I was by myself, alone in a caboose too tiny to even stand up straight in. My only company was a herd of thoroughly disinterested horses holding court in a nearby field. But if I squinted hard enough, I was back at Flathead Lake, in a warm semicircle of friends singing our hearts out and dreaming of a divinely inspired future. It wasn't until I drove back home at the end of the weekend that I realized what had happened. The reason I was so inspired that weekend was that I wasn't writing in public, trying to prove how much wiser I was than other White people. All weekend long, I thought about actual communities that friends of mine lived in and loved: about my college roommate Will, just an hour or so away in another tiny Iowa college town; about my closest friend from my TFA staff years, Lea in Memphis; about my nieces and nephews scattered across the country. I wasn't thinking about saving them or impressing them. I was just appreciative that they were out in the world, in communities that were not mine but that I cared about because of them.

I left that weekend with an embryonic idea, but it needed more work. For months, I hounded political organizers across the country, asking them to critique my theories as to how to train White people to talk to their neighbors. I asked friends and strangers alike to rip up holes in various drafts. I went to trainings. I developed a conversation model and practiced it over and over again. I knocked on doors, both on my own block and in neighborhoods thousands of miles away from mine. I coached liberal friends on how to talk to their Trump-loving grandparents, then anxiously awaited reports as to how the conversations went.

A year and a half later, in the early months of 2019, I finally felt confident enough in my idea to pitch it to donors.

I was armed with a long list of left-leaning foundations across the country and an equally expansive list of friends, mostly from TFA days, willing to connect me to them. I believed in what I was selling. Plus, I had a sense that the do-gooder foundation employees to whom I would be pitching would be particularly motivated by my ideas. I bet that Trump spooked them. How could he not have? Trump existed to spook the kind of people who worked at liberal foundations.

I was pretty damn confident. I'd put in the work. I'd met the moment with an inspired idea. I knew what I was doing.

And then I failed.

I failed in an office park in suburban Connecticut, after an extended conversation about how much I loved New Haven pizza. I failed in a hip foundation office in a former warehouse in Buffalo, a mirror image of the office I had just recently worked out of in Milwaukee. I failed in Minneapolis, Memphis, San Francisco, and back home in Milwaukee. Over the phone. In person. I failed with donors who stared me straight in the face and told me they didn't believe in my idea. I failed with donors who told me they loved it, that they were taking it immediately to their boards.

It was remarkable how much I was failing. I hadn't been all that skilled at fundraising back when I worked at TFA, but I at least scraped by. Back in those days, I pitched foundations right at the red-hot center of their White guilt pleasure centers. I went to most meetings with my then development director, Michelle, the Black woman from the north shore Milwaukee suburb, the one whom donors would ask whether she was grateful that her parents had traded a mostly Black community for a White one. We told them that neither they nor we were guilt-ridden saviors. We understood that what they cared about was empowerment, about investing in Milwaukee's youth as our future leaders.

Donors loved being told that they were in the empowerment business, especially when their money was going to communities that they associated with poverty and decay.

There was much less to love about my new pitch.

"Like, *which* White communities?"

"Do you mean, like, Appalachia?"

"Like a high-poverty community?"

Those questions soon became an expected feature of every meeting. No matter how progressive all these foundations claimed to be, they all operated in a similar paradigm. The logic of philanthropy is that there are two types of places in the world: communities that could give help and communities that needed help. The money came out of the first type of community and flowed to the second. The foundation staffers kept talking about Appalachia because that was the only type of White community they could imagine *needed* some sort of nonprofit intervention. Rednecks. Hillbillies. Waste people.

My problem was that I was selling something that their entire system couldn't digest. Why would I work in majority White communities like the ones all these foundation staffers lived in themselves? That wasn't where the work was. The problems were elsewhere.

I anticipated the question. But it took time to develop a good answer.

"Well, that's one area where I'd like to train organizers, yes, but I'm also excited to train White people in a variety of settings. For example, I'm interested in upper-middle-class White liberal parents who hold a lot of progressive beliefs but send their kids to private—"

"Well, thank you for your time. We'll get back to you in the next month or so . . . You know what would make us much more excited? I know that you're very committed to this whole 'White communities' thing, but have you considered bringing on a cofounder—a woman of color, specifically? And maybe offering corporate diversity trainings?"

I found myself moving further and further from that web of connection I wove when I was alone with my thoughts in that caboose. I stopped thinking about Jamie, my Tarkio-loving friend from high school. I stopped thinking about Emily, my ride-or-die companion at so many college protests, now a farmer in her hometown on the edge of Appalachian Ohio.

In every meeting, there was at least one besuited foundation executive who mentioned how concerned they were about the backward beliefs of rural, conservative White people.

"Have you read *Hillbilly Elegy*? Some of those communities are just so hopeless."

I nodded, smiled, and adapted my story. I talked more about Jefferson County, Montana, though not the relatively prosaic Jefferson County in which I actually grew up. I didn't talk about how my dad had a half-hour commute to an office building in Helena. I didn't talk about watching *E.T.* or playing *Burger Time*, because that would have painted Clancy as a place not too far removed from their own children's privileged, metropolitan upbringings.

Instead, I used the prejudices that were once the source of those excruciating Maryland stomachaches to my advantage. If upper-middle-class people were worried about the rednecks, and if those same people didn't know Clancy, Montana, from Harlan, Kentucky, then I had my ticket to riches. I wasn't too proud to pull out the rhetorical equivalent of overalls and a washboard and play them the old-timey small-town tune I believed they wanted to hear.

After the third or fourth meeting, I leaned hard into an exaggerated, cornpone story of Jefferson County. I threw out cherry-picked descriptors to signal to my audience that I grew up in the land of roughnecks and shitkickers whose voting habits were, at that point, the scourge of cosmopolitan dinner parties across the country.

I'd pilfer every story I once overheard from my older brothers about tough-guy brawlers from up in the hills who used to ride their high school bus. I remembered hearing about one guy who used to imitate the old commercial where a motorcycle revs through the countryside going, "*Raiiii-niieer Beeeer.*" He did that for the whole forty-five-minute ride from Clancy to Jefferson High School. I didn't really consider whether that story sounded more "annoying" than "hell-raising," but it was weird and off-kilter enough that the foundation officers' ears perked up when I told it.

My other favorite anecdotes concerned the radon health mines scattered in the hills between Boulder and Basin. The radon mines were exactly what they sounded like: former copper and silver shafts, long vacated but still full of extreme amounts of radon. A few decades ago, they were repurposed by enterprising entrepreneurs as health tourism destinations. Every day, a steady stream of mostly elderly seekers traveled to southern Jefferson County to sit in a tightly enclosed space and voluntarily subject themselves to the very same toxic chemical that middle-class metropolitan Americans pay to have removed from their basements.

"Can you believe it?" I asked my potential benefactors. "That's the kind of place I came from. Would you like to know the kind of names these places had?"

Of course they wanted to hear the names.

"So there's Earth Angel. But get this, another one is called Free Enterprise, but my favorite is called Merry Widow." I paused for their various "wows" and "I had no ideas."

The only way they could make sense of a place like Jefferson County was through paternalism. If my redneck backstory was convincing enough, perhaps there'd be a hefty grant waiting for me on the other side.

I felt guilty telling these stories. I'd repeat them in meetings and then retreat to the nearest restroom sink. I felt like I needed to throw up, but I never could. I heaved a little bit and then literally washed my hands of everything that had transpired in the previous hour. I couldn't imagine how my family, let alone anybody else from Jefferson County, would feel if they heard me in these meetings. The problem was, I didn't see any alternative. I believed in Barnraisers, but I couldn't do this work without funding, which meant that I had to flatter the sensibilities of people with power and money who I presumed, like me over the previous decade, cared more about the appearance of righteousness than the actual impact of their day jobs.

During this time, I checked in regularly with Isabella, June, and Barbara—three women (Latina, Asian, and Native, respectively) also in the process of launching nonprofits. We had met at one of those social entrepreneurship incubators and bonded over how little we wanted to prostrate ourselves for cash. These women, I learned, were doing their version of this same song and dance, painting two-dimensional portraits of their communities. We all felt unclean telling these stories, but none of us knew of an alternative.

PART SIX

Origin Story, Reprise

Chapter TWENTY-THREE

Perhaps I would have figured it out. Perhaps a few more months on the fundraising trail would have finally resulted in me hitting pay dirt.

I'll never know, though, because in late August 2019, the kids were asleep and Kjersti and I were sitting on the couch, half watching *The Bachelor*, half typing away at our laptops. One minute, I felt completely normal—tired, yes, and distracted by the fact that my big world-changing idea was still stuck in neutral, certainly, but normal. The next moment, everything changed. I was winded, sucking in more and more air, trying in vain to satiate myself. I felt like I needed desperately to lie down, even though I was already lying down. The room was spinning, even when I closed my eyes. I had not moved from the couch for nearly an hour, but it felt like I had just run a marathon and, as soon as I finished, a malevolent prankster spun me around a few times. My center, quite literally, wasn't holding.

I turned to Kjersti and explained what was happening.

Kjersti is a conscientious doctor, skilled in reading both symptoms and tone. Her voice was shaky, but both of us convinced ourselves that since all this came on so suddenly, it would clear up in time.

The next morning, the fog got worse. The thin summer sheet under which I slept weighed a thousand pounds. Soon, Kjersti was there by my side. She checked my heart rate. It was low, somewhere between twenty and thirty beats per minute.

Kjersti took the day off to accompany me to the emergency room. After a morning's worth of tests and a few minutes of staring at charts, the ER doctor admitted that she was as flummoxed as we were. As a consolation prize of sorts, she called in a young, green, visibly nervous physical therapist. It was immediately apparent that whatever textbooks he had studied in physical therapy school did not prepare him for whatever the hell was going on with me. After a long pause, he finally came up with an idea for a test.

"Would you mind shaking your head back and forth really fast?"

Skeptically, I followed his instructions.

"Okay, so how do you feel after shaking your head?"

"Still dizzy."

"Huh, that's interesting."

There were no further tests, nor any further diagnoses. He offered another "huh" as a parting gift, then promptly left the room. I was sent on my way.

Once home, I immediately crashed into bed. Kjersti's and my shared worry was now at a fever pitch. This was so sudden, so weird, and so unprecedented that every devastating outcome imaginable felt very real.

The counterpoint to all these worries was that just as every worst-case scenario was possible, so too was every best case. This could have just been psychosomatic. But not knowing terrified me. I hadn't had a doctor tell me that they couldn't explain what was wrong with me since those childhood stomachaches.

Unlike my childhood, I now had to get out of bed, go downstairs to my children, and admit that Daddy was sick and that we didn't know why. I had to half-truthfully answer a couple of follow-up questions from Olof, who, at six years old, already knew that when you received unexpected news, the next step was to watch your parents' faces for clues to triage the level of worry you're supposed to have. I explained to them that I couldn't play Monster Chase or give them the wild knee-top horse rides that they loved. I was too tired.

For the next two to three months, every day was the same. I woke up and immediately felt like I needed to go back to sleep. I did my best to help the kids with their morning routine, but the sheer energy expenditure of doing so required me to lie down or take a bath for four to five hours. That would then take me to late afternoon, where I'd repeat the cycle: try to make dinner, try to play with the kids, and collapse back into bed when it all became too much. It didn't take long before I exhausted the variety of games that I could play with Ida and Olof while lying down. I became a master at variations of "sleeping giant," "introverted troll," and, when I didn't even have the energy to wake up and wave my arms, "mountain" or "pile of dirt."

I did the bare minimum when it came to entertaining my children, just as I did the bare minimum at just about everything. All the rhythms of daily life fell by the wayside: work, of course, but also cooking, cleaning, grocery shopping, chauffeuring the children, etc. None of that work disappeared. It fell on Kjersti, who also took on the extra weight of worrying about me. This was her field! If there was an answer out there for me, she should have had access to it. But she didn't, which meant that she was left with the implication of all that not knowing. If she didn't know the answer, and if other doctors didn't have the answer, then perhaps there was no answer.

So Kjersti fretted and picked up my slack. I, in turn, felt terrible but literally didn't have the energy to do anything about it. Whatever story I told myself about our partnership—about how I was a great male feminist partner and co-parent—was clearly a lie.

What I did have energy for was staring at screens, so that's what I did. I watched every Marvel movie in order, mostly because there were so many of them and I had the time.

I quickly discovered that the Marvel movies, especially when watched in succession, were fine. They were all a blur of punches and explosions and characters, whose names sometimes included definite articles. There were quips. So many quips. "That'll leave a mark!" "So that happened!" etc. etc. It took me less than a week before I realized that I had watched the same story told with a dozen different accents. It was one facsimile of a Joseph Campbell narrative after another, tales of otherwise unexceptional White men whose lives become interesting only when something mysterious and cataclysmic happens to their bodies. *Good for them,* I thought. At least their ailments transformed them into superheroes.

The parts of these movies to which I could fully relate were the scenes in which various scientists and doctors stared at our hero's transformed body and remarked that they'd "never seen anything like this!" I relived those scenes quite a bit that fall. I bounced between medical office buildings across the county, seeing different neurologists, pulmonologists, and cardiologists. I received CAT scans and X-rays and stress tests and exhausted my reserve of novel ways to explain to nurses that the room in which we were both sitting was spinning around rapidly. I clutched the sides of too many sticky plastic hospital chairs. But still, I heard disbelief in their voices.

"That just doesn't make sense."

My stress test at the cardiologist's office was a highlight, if only because I got to use a treadmill. The medical assistant who helped me out, professional and courteous the whole time, loaded me up with wires and informed me in a heavy Wisconsin accent that I should tell her immediately if and when I got dizzy.

"Okay, now."

"What do you mean?"

"I'm already dizzy, like, now."

Visibly confused, she paused for a beat. "Um, do you still want to do this?"

"I mean, might as well."

She let me run until we both got bored. Every ten seconds or so, she asked me if I was still dizzy. I gave her a thumbs-up. At some arbitrary point, she stopped the treadmill and I got off. A few weeks later, her boss, the cardiologist, informed me with clear disinterest that there was nothing wrong with my heart and, therefore, nothing he could do for me.

Chapter TWENTY-FOUR

During the three months when I was bedridden, I cycled through a whole catalog's worth of emotions. I was angry. I was perplexed. I was overwhelmed with marital guilt and worries of professional failure (it goes without saying that I made no progress on Barnraisers fundraising). I'd spent an entire lifetime telling myself that I would be okay if I was perceived as being good for others, and here I was, doing absolutely nothing.

And then, after about two months, after all the other emotions were exhausted, I finally just felt sorry for myself—without caveat, without immediately chasing it with faux self-aware acknowledgment that I had no right to pity myself because of my relative privilege. I was going through a legitimately frustrating experience. I was both sick and lonely. The people who were supposed to help did not understand me. And it was okay for me to neither over- nor understate that feeling.

I practiced saying it out loud:

"I wish this hadn't happened to me."

That's all. Nothing more, nothing less. I finally allowed myself to admit that nobody, myself included, enjoyed feeling sick and misunderstood.

It wasn't until I started saying it out loud that I realized I had been here before. This was exactly how I felt in third grade, when the teachers thought I was a dumb hick and none of the doctors could figure out the cause of my stomachaches. I wished that too hadn't happened.

I had skipped this step, even now that I was no longer rejecting other White people, even now that I felt like I had finally given up the religion of being right for the religion of being in love. I would have sworn I hadn't skipped this step—the one that involved loving myself enough to afford myself sympathy without caveat. I would have claimed for decades that my problem was that I was *too* in love with myself. Wasn't that why I craved positions of visibility and power? I didn't notice that I had spent my whole adult life believing that I deserved sympathy and love only if I was less racist than the other Whites, only if the right kind of people admired me, only if I was useful.

Earlier that summer, I got a message from James, one of my primary teenage nemeses, saying that he hoped I could make it to our twentieth high school reunion. It was the kind of note you write when you were once a tough teenager with a lot of bravado and no small dose of meanness, but only because you struggled with a lot of things that you weren't able to talk about at the time. It was the kind of letter you send when you're proud of the life you've lived, the lessons you've learned, the kind of dad you are to your daughters, but you've also got some regrets and you'd like to set things right before the Loyola Sacred Heart Class of 1999 gathers together at a moderately fancy bar and grill on Brooks Street.

I hovered over the message before building up the courage to click on it. I was a thirty-eight-year-old man, but seeing James's name on my screen made me feel sixteen. I feared imminent mockery, as if somehow the electronic message itself would reach out and shove me against a locker. Once I finally opened it, I couldn't believe what I read. It wasn't just that it was kind. It was regretful, proud, and hoping for reconnection. I smiled a big, goofy, face-widening smile and reread it. First once, then twice, then three times.

James admitted that we both didn't really know each other. How could we have? We hadn't really known ourselves. I replied graciously, expressing regret and what I hoped was a sincere note of gratitude for the fact that he reached out to me. I told him I felt sorry as well, that I had made a caricature of him too.

"I wish this hadn't happened to me."

"I wish this didn't happen to anybody."

For once, I was ready to tell an honest story of the radon health mines of Jefferson County, Montana.

Those mines weren't really punch lines. They were real spaces. Hopeful spaces. They were filled with the zeal of people taking one last wild chance. They were frequented by old people who were at the end of their rope—seniors who suffered from chronic pain: arthritis, macular degeneration, ankylosing spondylitis, cancer. The kind of person who descended into a radon mine, who packed a sweater to ward against the subterranean chill and cribbage boards to stave off boredom, was somebody who had already tried everything. They were tired of doctors not having any useful advice, tired of feeling like their bodies were at war with them.

You don't descend into a cave if you're confident that the world above ground will welcome and embrace you. You don't drink radioactive water by the bucketful and take deep breaths of radioactive air and rub radioactive mud all over your aching joints if all the conventional right answers haven't already failed you.

———

As I lay in bed every day, the reconsiderations flowed in and out of each other. By now I had half-consciously added a couple of new mantras to my repertoire. I didn't realize that they were prayers.

"I just want somebody to understand me."

The more I repeated the phrase, the more I noticed that I already had people around me trying to do precisely that, not the least of which was my family doctor, Mary, who thought about me daily. She was the one recommending that laundry list of physicians. Eventually, after so many false starts with so many cocky male specialists, she asked me to meet with a vestibular physical therapist named Sarah.

Sarah couldn't figure out what was wrong with me but

was so puzzled and eager to help that she called her colleagues for advice on my behalf. One of those colleagues believed that, while it normally didn't cause acute symptoms this dramatic, exploring the possibility of sleep apnea was worth a shot.

Mary's curiosity begot Sarah's curiosity, which begot her colleague's curiosity, and soon I was standing in front of a sleep study technician named Beth in yet another anonymous medical office building in the suburbs south of Milwaukee. Beth didn't have to let me in when she did; yes, she had a cancellation, but she could have just gifted herself with a lighter night. But when I explained my mysterious symptoms over the phone, she was curious. She wanted to see if she could help.

I arrived at the office and was greeted warmly by Beth, who took me to the mini hotel suite they had in the back and loaded me up with what felt like fifty little taped-on plugs and electrodes and wires. Those wires were then affixed to a small rectangular box, which I toted around like a Merry Mouse on the first day of kindergarten. I looked like a poorly constructed child's Halloween costume of a robot. I was overjoyed.

This was now all that I wanted. I wanted a stranger named Beth to care about what was wrong with me. I called Kjersti, her voice filled with a lightness and ebullience I hadn't heard for months. I called my parents, who sounded near tears.

I turned on the TV, eventually landing on a Ken Burns documentary on PBS about country music. That night, the narrator talked about how Hank Williams was both a rare talent and a sad, self-destructive morphine and booze addict. He was beloved by millions, but it didn't matter. A few months earlier, I would have argued that Williams wasn't deserving of my sympathy because he was a privileged thief. One day, he had just been a kid from Alabama hanging around with a guitar, and then he ran into a Black blues musician with the all-time great name of Tee-Tot Payne who taught him everything he knew. Fast-forward a few years, and Williams was the biggest country music star ever. I knew to sneer at this kind of story: the older Black guy teaches the younger White guy the blues, the White guy gets famous, and the Black guy dies penniless. What ingratitude. What blatant cultural appropriation. And what did the rich and famous White guy do? He drowned himself in booze and pills and whined about how lonesome he was all the time.

That's all true. But it was never that simple. Hank Williams may have sung about being lonesome and sad, but that wasn't his real problem. His real problem was that he was in chronic pain. He had an undiagnosed case of spina bifida; he was being attacked by his own spinal cord. To deal with the pain, he turned to booze and drugs, the latter of which was supplied to him by a con artist masquerading as a physician, Dr. Lemon. I suspect that Williams wasn't crying because he was lonesome, though if he were that would have been a decent excuse, even for a famous country star. He was crying because he had to choose between being drugged up and famous or dope sick and immobile.

After about a half hour of feeling sympathy for Hank Williams, the documentary concluded, and I pressed the intercom button to tell Beth that I was going to sleep and that, through the magic of all those wires, she could finally crack the case of what had been ailing me.

I was barely asleep for a couple of hours before Beth's voice came over my in-room intercom to inform me, with some urgency, that we needed to get me breathing on a CPAP machine. Apparently, the maze of wires told her how frequently I was going through the classic sleep apneic cycle of choking, brain panicking, and waking myself up. The answer was, per Beth, "way, way too much"—more than sixty times an hour. When I woke up in the morning, I had likely been masked up and breathing mechanically for a third of the night, but I felt wildly and uncommonly well rested.

"Wait," I told Beth as she helped me unplug the tangle of cords, "so you're telling me it's normal to wake up and not immediately feel like you could sleep for another eight hours?"

She laughed politely. She had seen scores of grateful non-sleepers have these little epiphanies. Her initial sympathy and curiosity on the phone had continued over the course of my visit. Beth was a true believer in the power of sleep studies, and while my symptoms seemed more sudden and dramatic than those of most others with sleep apnea, she'd crossed her fingers that one night in her care could unlock everything for me.

After that first decent night's sleep, I still had to wait—first for a CPAP machine to become available, and then to have enough nights with it for it to start making a difference. I also wasn't done with my various visits to befuddled specialists. The diagnosis explained a lot, but not everything. It explained why I'd been so tired over the past decade, but not why that fatigue had manifested in sudden, acute symptoms.

I never got a full answer to that question, though I spent enough time with an ear, nose, and throat doctor to discover that if I flushed my sinuses daily and slept religiously with the CPAP, the dizziness eventually became a rare occurrence rather than a normal one. When people ask me what ailment I have, I usually mumble something about sinusitis and sleep apnea, but really, I'm still not sure. I just know that for a while my body wasn't mine, and now, if I do specific things, it mostly is again.

There was part of me that was embarrassed that my grand mystery illness was this banal. Sinusitis and sleep apnea? That's not special. There are ads for CPAPs on cable news. I made Kjersti go through all of that—the fear, the doctors' visits, the childcare and housework burden—for an ailment that everybody's dad seems to have.

All that's true. Whether fair or not, that guilt is real. But what's also true is that another way of saying "not special" is "not alone."

Chapter TWENTY-FIVE

It took getting sick to get over myself, at least a bit. For years, I told the story that being a Bucks was an inheritance I had to earn, a legacy I had to live up to. I couldn't imagine that I could receive a gift without there being an obligation. And it took getting over myself to realize that I had been telling myself stories for years—stories about myself, for sure, but stories more about my family.

After I got sick, though, I asked my parents to tell me more about those early years of starting their marriage.

After that night in August 1968, the one where the cops beat up the hippies and the kids chanted "The whole world is watching!" and my idealistic father sat in a tiny living room in Brookings, South Dakota, cursing a country that would take away Martin and Bobby and leave us only with Hubert Humphrey—Dan Bucks had to wake up the next morning.

More specifically, he had to get back to work. That fall, he traveled around the state as Humphrey's South Dakota campaign director. He visited little towns like Doland, giving his all for a candidate who wasn't Bobby Kennedy, but whom he still believed in. Both of my parents worked hard to get Humphrey elected. It wasn't enough—Lyndon Johnson's war was too unpopular, Nixon's bag of dirty campaign tricks too deep—so the morning after Election Day they woke up and once again got back to work.

A few years and a number of jobs later, my parents worked equally tirelessly on Dick Kneip's campaign for governor. Kneip was one more small-town populist—originally from Salem, another highway dot, this one between Sioux Falls and Mitchell—in the Henry Wallace, Hubert Humphrey, and George McGovern tradition. That time around, all the work paid off, and in 1972 both the Kneip and the Bucks families moved to the state capital of Pierre.

Kneip's victory meant there was even more work to be done. Not star-making work, but important work nonetheless. My family—my mom, my dad, Eric, Colin, and Brian—moved to a little rental home within walking distance of the capitol, and they met another political couple with a big gaggle of kids, the McKeevers, who would become their lifelong friends. My dad, twenty-seven years old and with all the professional energy in the world, led a tremendously unsexy but important reorganization of the South Dakota government. He and my mom would discuss political strategy at night, and then he'd head back to the capitol building in the morning with my mother's ideas fresh in his head. My mother led La Leche League meetings for breastfeeding mothers and worked on political campaigns and watched as her boys and the McKeever kids—now eight strong with the birth of my brother Nate—ping-ponged between each other's houses. On weekend nights, my folks would pack up the whole crew and tromp them over to the governor's mansion to babysit Dick Kneip's family as well.

My self-mythologizing stories notwithstanding, my parents never felt their dreams or ambitions were dashed by parenthood. My mother loved both her self-directed experiment in feminist boy-raising and the opportunity that her partnership with my dad gave her to influence state politics. My father, in turn, was deeply proud of delivering exactly what he promised when he came to work for the state. His government reorganization plan was necessary to move the state away from some old cronyistic laws that favored railroads and agribusiness companies over working-class South Dakotans.

Around the time Dick Kneip left South Dakota for an ambassadorship, my father received a scholarship from the Bush Foundation for a master's in public administration. The award was supposed to enable him to move the family to one of the meccas for political strivers, Harvard or Stanford. He called them back and asked, at my mother's urging, if they'd allow him to use the scholarship to attend the University of Montana in Missoula instead.

Jane Bucks's determination to make our family Montanans was a statement of values and principles as clear as any minister-poet's confirmation class exhortation. Whenever there was a choice to be made, my parents chose to commit to a specific place. Over the years, they continued their pattern of doing the work they could to help those places be a little kinder and more loving. My mother worked at a home for teenage mothers in crisis in Helena and helped found a whole system of neighborhood councils in Missoula. My father served on the Clancy school board and spent years studying the Montana tax code, closing loopholes that kept millionaires from sharing their money with schoolteachers and families on welfare. They did all that wherever they lived, but they especially did it in Montana.

Contrary to my puffed-up narrative of family legacies deferred, Evelyn and George Gelston and Vera and Russell Bucks didn't teach their kids to fight the world's injustices because they needed our family tree to create a hero. They wanted their kids to do exactly what my parents ended up doing: commit to a community, care about that community, work tirelessly in that community.

As for Ken, my mom kept her promise to him as well. That promise wasn't to ensure that one of her boys reached the heights to which he may or may not have scaled in his life. It was simply to never stop being his adoring kid sister. That's why we were Montanans, after all. We weren't Montanans because the size of its sky inspires overwrought elegies or because its tallest mountains threaten to scrape the heavens. We were Montanans because that's where Ken will forever be, somewhere in the ice-cold waters of the St. Mary River, somewhere below the mountain trails his little sister still hikes every summer, keeping his memory alive.

Chapter TWENTY-SIX

T hroughout those years after Trump's election, first when I was developing and pitching Barnraisers, and then when I was sick in bed, I still sought out White heroes. Perhaps there will be a day in the future when I can fully say to myself, *Garrett, this is how you walk in the world—it has its strengths, it has its limitations, but it is your specific, unique walk, and it does not require you to shadow somebody else's.* Perhaps someday, but up to this point, not yet.

It's telling that even in that moment, when I sought White role models who organized other White people, I still wanted to make sure that I picked somebody who was officially endorsed and validated by Black people. The full extent of my 'rigorous "find a White hero" research method was to open up the section of Martin Luther King Jr.'s letter from Birmingham Jail where he rattled off a list of White people he admired and then google their names.

I knew this list existed because, over the course of the previous decade, I had read the letter at least a half dozen times.

This was a sacred text in the religion of being right, or at least in that church's Whiter congregations. Back when I worked in education, I heard the same Dr. King quotes about "White moderates" hurled back and forth between lefty union activists and libertarian school choice acolytes, each side pretending that they were the first ones to wield the text like a weapon, each pretending that the same lines hadn't just been directed their way. I once listened to a fiery speech by a White celebrity superintendent who claimed that he reread it every Sunday night. I went home and tried to re-create the ritual myself, but fell asleep after a few pages.

While I didn't read King's letter from Birmingham Jail every Sunday night, I read it enough times that I knew there was a list of MLK-approved White people in there. That's how I found Anne Braden.

It's an imperfect discovery story, but it is honest. And however sweaty the process that led to my first encounter with Anne Braden may have been, I found her right on time. Braden, an Alabama-raised, Louisville-based activist from the 1950s all the way to the early aughts, lived the life I now imagined for myself. She spent a lifetime traveling the South organizing White people—many of them poor—for social justice movements. But she also spent a lifetime talking about her Whiteness out loud, not in the way I used to in my social media diatribes, but in a manner that was much more vulnerable, much more welcoming.

Braden had a lot of stories. The one that stuck with me

the most took place in Birmingham in the 1940s. Braden was a young newspaper reporter covering the court beat. She already considered herself a civil rights liberal by that point—a series of progressive pastors and influential college professors had helped her reject her parents' Jim Crow politics.

One morning, she stopped by the county courthouse to see if there were any cases noteworthy enough to require her to rush to the office to type up an article for the evening edition. Afterward, she met up with a White friend at a downtown diner for breakfast. Braden's friend inquired as to whether she had received a juicy tip.

"No, just a colored murder," Braden replied absentmindedly, before realizing that not only had their Black waitress overheard the remark, but that she (the waitress) "was pouring coffee into our cups and her hand was sort of shaking, but there wasn't an expression on her face. It was like she had a mask."

Now noticing the waitress—which is to say, noticing the waitress notice her—Braden immediately went into fix-it mode.

In Braden's recollection, "my first impulse was that I wanted to get up and go put my arms around her and say, 'Oh I'm sorry. I didn't mean that.'"

It's a painfully honest story. Had the Black waitress not appeared by Braden's side, she wouldn't have even remembered the incident. It wasn't guilt or complicity Anne Braden felt in that moment. It was isolation, nakedness. She sensed that her mistake separated herself from the Black waitress, and she craved an immediate cleanse through physical touch and proximity. She needed to hug the waitress, which is to say that she needed, desperately, for the waitress to embrace her.

I recognized that impulse, the reaching out for the hug, the hope that if you can just receive the perfect piece of Black or Brown affirmation, all your exposed racism will melt away.

I read Anne Braden's story in February 2020. It arrived in my life right on time, both at the exact moment when I was finally ready to hear it and immediately before the swirl of the world around me would make its message particularly prescient. Had all the national and international events of 2020 occurred just a few years earlier, or even a few months earlier, I would have viewed it as my moment to finally emerge as a *movement leader*, attempting to write the most strident, viral essays that White America had ever read. I would have sneered at everything White people were or weren't doing around me. I would have done anything and everything to stand out.

As it turns out, it takes more than a thoughtful mother's intentional feminist messaging to keep the White guy from shoving himself to the front of the line. In my case, it took being stripped of so many presumed birthrights of White maleness: a cascade of effortless professional success, a body that didn't make me feel weak, and freedom from workday childcare responsibilities.

Two of those three shoes had already dropped for me before the spring of 2020. It took the world shutting down for the COVID-19 pandemic for the final one to drop as well.

The part of my brain that had desired to save the world was finally quieted, muffled underneath piles of laundry and disinfectant wipes and my jury-rigged attempts to hastily replicate a trimester's worth of first-grade instruction. I shuttled my kids to literally every single public forest in Milwaukee County, fretted about what Kjersti might be encountering at the hospital, and went grocery shopping in apocalyptically bare-shelved stores after my family members were safely in bed. I'd avoid eye contact as I checked out, unsure whether too heavy an exchange of empathy might unleash the plague.

I was tired and stressed but also delighted in all this time I got with my kids, particularly after my illness. Ida was three now, no longer a baby, confident and clever and pound for pound the strongest member of our family unit. Olof was almost seven, empathetic and old enough to process the world around him. I loved their laughs. I loved seeing every emotion expressed vividly in their big perfect eyes.

All three of us were proud of Kjersti. Neither she nor her colleagues deserved this disaster, but I was so grateful knowing that it was her who was taking care of our city's babies and grandparents during such an unfathomably frightening time.

Some nights I wrote, but they weren't jeremiads anymore. I wasn't as interested in lecturing. I cared much more about no longer being alone.

This was the shape of my life when, on May 25, a Minneapolis cop named Derek Chauvin strangled a Black man, George Floyd, to death. This was the shape of my life when

first thousands and then millions of White people started re-
acting to Floyd's murder, when the largest crowd I had ever
seen gathered in Milwaukee marched by my house on a daily
basis, when every single headline in every news outlet was
about racial justice, when a million strident statements and
manifestos were issued by a million strident White people.

At one point in that fever dream of a summer, windows
were smashed and fires were set not far from my house. The
kids and I were on our way to a park the morning after a particularly volatile night had settled into a tense, muggy day;
we saw a crowd of White anarchists in matching black hood-
ies skirting in and out of alleys, not far from the rubble of
burned-out buildings.

At another point that summer, there was a march in Aberdeen, South Dakota, of all places. Aberdeen wasn't Doland,
but it was close. It was the town where my mother was born,
where she and Ken caught the train to Glacier National Park
every summer. A crowd of a few dozen, most of them teens,
waved signs and chanted as the sun set on a June prairie evening. Their twin single-file lines were long enough to stretch
multiple blocks of Sixth Avenue, from Kusler's gas station/
casino all the way to the Methodist church. A picture in the
Aberdeen News showed a group of young White women holding signs. They were dressed in shorts and sandals, their ex-
pressions uncomfortable, a product of either deep solemnity
or sticky summer heat.

On one sign: I UNDERSTAND THAT I WILL NEVER UNDER-
STAND HOWEVER I STAND.

Another: I'M NOT BLACK BUT I SEE YOU. I'M NOT BLACK BUT I HEAR YOU. I'M NOT BLACK BUT I MOURN FOR YOU. I'M NOT BLACK BUT I WILL FIGHT FOR YOU.

There were layers to those signs, I imagined. Conviction, yes, but also hesitancy. A preemptive apology. A raised voice, but with a slight stutter.

Many days, I felt the familiar drag toward judgment and exceptionalism. At one point, a picture circulated of former Republican presidential candidate Mitt Romney marching in a Salt Lake City protest. There was nothing in Romney's adult career that spoke of a deep commitment to racial justice. Had my motivations over the course of all these years been empathetic, rooted in a dream of progress toward liberation for all, nothing about Mitt Romney saying "Black Lives Matter" should have bothered me. But those had never been my sole motivations, so of course it took me aback, if only for a second, to be no more cleansed of the sins of Whiteness than Mitt Romney of all people.

What was different in 2020 was that I finally noticed my judgment. I understood *why* I craved separation from all the White people around me. I also noticed for the first time that I wasn't the only White person driven to separate myself from the pack. Romney wanted to make clear that he may have been in the streets, but he wasn't a violent radical. The black-clad anarchists wanted to make it equally clear that, for them, the opposite was true. Those young people in Aberdeen likely wanted to take a stand, but didn't want anybody to get mad at them for saying the wrong thing. Friends across the country who used to shout "Black Lives Matter" suddenly felt that slogan wasn't radical enough; they now called for defunding the police. I trusted the earnestness of their convictions; I held those beliefs as well. I also recognized, however, the gift of that rhetorical radicalism for our troubled souls. We believed what we were saying, but that didn't mean we didn't also take comfort in knowing that there were other White people for whom that was a bridge too far.

We were all Anne Braden, reaching out to that waitress, praying that she'd hug us back.

I spent that summer watching White people more intently than I ever had before. I wasn't waiting for my turn at the megaphone. By the time June became July, I noticed the distinct presence of an emotion that I had honestly never felt toward other White people, which is to say that I had never felt it when I noticed my own Whiteness.

It was tenderness.

It was affection.

It was an actual desire for connection—not to save, not to be saved, but just to be a member of a community.

I felt responsibility for both the mess that the great White "we" had made as well as our dizzy, fumbling attempts to find a way through. I felt a desire to push and critique those look-at-me anarchists, those shame-filled middle managers writing hollow statements for multinational corporations, those sheltered Aberdeenians, even Mitt Romney, but no longer as artificially distanced adversaries. What's more, I was open to all of them potentially pushing and critiquing me.

What a mess we were, us White people. And of course. We had no reason to be anything but a mess. We had no experience—this ragtag assortment of people who once had ethnic identities but were now more or less just White—being anything but a mess. And here we were, this summer, being so clearly messy in public. We were reaching out, all of us, for some version of an embrace. All those who marched, all those who smashed windows, all those who *tsk-tsk*ed the marchers and smashers alike and who would, one summer later, vote for "law and order" candidates and demand that their local school board ban "critical race theory" books. We were all doing the same thing: noticing our Whiteness, hating how alone it made us feel, wishing that somebody or something could make it all disappear.

What a mess! What a cataclysmic, selfish, violent, death-causing mess! What a domination-enabling mess! What a much-too-large-and-tangled-for-any-one-of-us-to-figure-out-alone mess!

What a gift, then, that it wasn't my mess to clean up alone. It was ours, together.

It was around that time that we were able to figure out what childcare looked like in an age of COVID, which meant that I finally had time to make a public offering to all the earnest White seekers around me.

I spent a couple of weeks dusting off my now fallow plans to train other White people on how to organize their communities for justice. I kept the Barnraisers name, but it was no longer the grand, quick-scaling nonprofit empire that I had once pitched. It was now just a simple set of trainings. I'd offer them online and make them available to anybody who wanted to show up. If they found it useful, I'd ask for a donation at the end to keep it going. If they didn't find it useful, I'd welcome their feedback. If they finished the training and actually started a political organizing effort, I'd offer whatever support they needed and desired. The trainings were deliberately joyful rather than funereal. I didn't lecture, and I wouldn't let the participants compete with one another to prove whose politics were most above reproach. We laughed hard, and often.

There's a longer story to be told about these organizing cohorts. There's a story about how quickly I found, basically through word of mouth, first dozens, then hundreds, and eventually more than a thousand White people who were craving something similar to me. There is a story to tell about all the stories and communities I discovered through these cohorts, about how I'd spend an afternoon on the phone to New Orleans one minute and western Iowa the next, to a seventeen-year-old in Manhattan for the first half of an hour and a seventy-year-old in the Palouse Valley of Idaho for the second half. There's a story about all the questions I discovered that my trainings still don't answer, like how to find the time to organize, or how to meet your neighbors in a world where most of our muscles for neighborliness have atrophied, or whether training a hundred White people at a time with no rigorous accountability for what they do after that training really makes a difference.

It's not that these stories don't matter, but it's difficult to tell them without leaning back into faux-authoritative lectures and other tools of the religion of being right. Like all of us, I'm still discovering what it looks like to balance my ego, to stand for something while not letting judgments stand in the way of connection. Every conversation, every relationship, every new organizing effort is a gift, though. Every one reveals a bit more of the path. A book has an ending. A life spent in the religion of love is much more of an ellipsis.

There are still so many questions to answer. And thank goodness. Because if there is one thing I've discovered for certain, it's that I no longer want to puzzle through them by myself.

EPILOGUE

In June 2022, I finally visited Doland. I had never been there as an adult, not once in all those years of claiming to be haunted by the place.

I was on my way to Butte, Montana, for a writing residency. Doland is a nine-and-a-half-hour drive from Milwaukee, and I got into town right around dusk. The sign on the edge of town welcomed me to THE HOME OF HEROES.

I parked my car and walked the two blocks of downtown, snapping pictures to send to my parents. I strolled down Humphrey Drive, the renamed Main Street that was once home to my grandmother's library and my grandfather's service station. I passed the still formidable grain elevator and the long-shuttered Twin Kiss Theatre. As far as midwestern towns go, it felt neither noticeably affluent nor impoverished. It just felt small. Smaller than it used to be, to be sure, but far from dead. The sky was a gorgeous pink, the East River flatness offering the gift of a horizon that seemed like it would never end.

A couple of older guys spotted me and gestured to meet them at their perch in front of the senior center. They introduced themselves as Bill and Gene and offered me friendly but slightly suspicious handshakes. Understandably, they wanted to know what I was doing skulking around town taking pictures. I told them that my folks grew up here: Dan Bucks and Jane Gelston.

Their faces lit up. Sure, they remembered the Gelstons and the Buckses! Soon they were regaling me with stories of my relatives. "Oh yeah, Vera? The last time we saw her was on the party bus we all booked to Branson, Missouri."

Well played, Grandma Vera. She never told any of us about a party bus.

I mentioned Ken, but the name didn't really register for them. Bill and Gene were younger than my parents, closer in age to my father's kid sister, Karen, and my mother's sisters, Sally and Kay. The names that mattered to them weren't abstract tragic legends but the actual people they knew, their old friends and classmates.

I asked a lot of questions about the town. My suspicions were correct: Doland was trucking along, neither thriving nor flailing. It still had the school and the church. The bar and grill on Main Street was doing okay. It had been a decent year for the farmers who were still carrying on; it's just that there were a whole lot less of them than there once were. Bill and Gene remembered when everything started changing, not long after my grandfathers' deaths. The tractors got bigger, the profit margins got tighter, and what was once was a patch-work of small farms was consolidated into a few behemoth operations.

I asked them how they felt about all that, and they shrugged. "What are you gonna do, you know?"

They asked me why I had come through town, and I mentioned the writing residency and the fact that I was work-ing on a book.

"What's it about?"

I gulped. "You know, it's a story about me, believe it or not," I replied nervously. "Turns out, I spent a whole lot of my life trying to prove that I was better than everybody else. I'm pretty passionate about politics. You know, I'm pretty far on the left—my family always was . . ."

They nodded, perhaps out of politeness, perhaps out of recognition.

"What I've come to realize, though, is that it didn't matter how loudly I could yell at everybody I disagreed with. That didn't make the world better. I skipped a step. I never learned how to actually be a part of a community."

As soon as the words left my mouth, I doubted them. That description felt simultaneously too vague and too revealing. I wondered whether I should have been more direct, if I should have initiated a conversation about antiracism and Trump. Wasn't that what my Barnraisers cohorts were all about? Was I a coward for not playing all my cards? Or should I have gone the other way? I mean, they weren't really interested in an honest answer. I could have said, "Oh yeah, I'm writing my life's story."

I filtered through a hundred assumptions about Bill and Gene. I bet they were MAGA guys. I bet they hated me and the Toyota Prius I rode in on. I didn't know any of that, of course, and I definitely hadn't asked. For all my desire to reach out and build bridges, I wasn't above feeling jittery and judgy in moments such as this.

Bill responded, granting me a reprieve from my self-flagellation:

"Yeah, I think you're onto something with that. Community. I bet you've heard from your folks, but we used to have a lot more of that here than we do now."

Afterword

At the beginning of this book, I promised that I would tell a single story about how Whiteness reacts when it sees itself in the mirror. Telling that story required excavating both the moments when I tried to distinguish myself from other White people as well as why it felt so urgent to do so. I had to consider what about my own Whiteness felt as if it were only metabolizable through guilt and shame. I was honest about where that left me—isolated, ineffective and with very little to show for all of my strident political opinions.

I honestly didn't know how other White people would react to my story when I published it. While I've been immensely lucky to receive a wide variety of responses—including from, as I hoped, others willing to share their stories of being the right kind of White—one of the most common refrains has been less of a comment than a question.

"But how do I actually do this 'not running away from other White people' thing?"

I've got nothing against clear instructions. But if there's one truth that I've discovered the hard way, it's that concrete advice is only useful if you're open to taking it. In many ways, this book was an outgrowth of the trainings I run with the Barnraisers Project. Though I adore those trainings, there is no magic to them. The actions I encourage participants to take are both simple and intuitive. You pay attention to local news, not for the salacious headlines but to learn who in your midst is already engaged in caring, connective work. You log onto city council meetings and make note of what issues are galvanizing your neighbors. You start showing up in a way that works for your ability level and welcome friends to join you. When you have a conversation with somebody who does not already share all of your political commitments, you lead with curiosity rather than righteous fury. You trust more in the transformative power of relationships than rhetoric.

I truly believe those are all useful lessons, but in my experience, it didn't matter how many workshops I attended or how many books I read. I wasn't ready for the work of community transformation if I hadn't gone through the kind of generous-but-clear-eyed self-reflection that I hope you've seen modeled in this book. I needed to interrogate what about my path through life pulled me toward the religion of being right rather than the religion of being in love. Without that step, I kept falling back into the trap of ego-gratification and puffery.

That's all to say, I'm still resisting the urge to end this book with a checklist. What I'll offer instead is one last story. Putting a book into the world is, at its core, an invitation to be in conversation with others, and for me that's meant meeting groups from across the country who are imagining a different way of being in community with other White people.

None of these groups were founded by professional organizers—they were people who, like me, craved an alternative to the politics of self-righteousness. They were moms in a tony, majority-White section of Minneapolis, the kind of neighborhood that progressive activists often deride as only being interested in protecting their own wealth and privilege. They were citizen activists in rural Washington who dreamed that they could convince their entire state—from Seattle to the Scablands—to vote for universal healthcare. They were once-disconnected neighbors in Lynchburg, Virginia, who were fed up with a city council that spent its time on reactionary culture war nonsense rather than fixing the city streets. I talked with them in barns and bars and Quaker meetinghouses and virtual Zoom rooms. I heard about their victories and their setbacks.

In each place, their story was the same as mine. They had to give up the narcotizing myth that, by running away from White people in their communities, they could transcend to some higher plane of Whiteness. That choice was hard, but the steps that followed weren't. In very different contexts, they all asked their neighbors, essentially "want to work on something that would improve our community?" and they were met with plenty of raised hands.

And no, none of these plucky little organizing efforts have single-handedly saved Whiteness from itself. But here's what has changed in my own life, thanks in part to my now constantly outstretched hand. Just about every day now, I get to meet a once-stranger who also believes that their little corner of White America can change—that it might vote differently or become more welcoming to its neighbors. And with every new conversation, I become further convinced that, when our hearts are ready, we don't need a checklist.

Acknowledgments

I am grateful. So grateful. I am grateful not just for all those who have contributed to this book, but for the various intersecting communities that have shaped me. If this book is about abandoning the myth that mine was ever an individual hero's journey, then the greatest gift of this process was being reminded, again and again, that all projects are group projects.

Thank you . . .

To my editor, Yahdon Israel, for pushing, prodding, and trusting that I had this narrative inside me. You offered me all your heart and mind and cared for/fretted about every word on these pages as much as I did. As a token of my gratitude, I've tried to make it through this paragraph without any adverbs.

To the entire team at Simon & Schuster who contributed to *The Right Kind of White*, for your attention, creativity, and talent: Sophia Benz, Jackie Seow, Lewelin Polanco, Danielle Preilipp, Martha Langford, Julia Prosser, Jonathan Evans, Allison Har-zvi, Amanda Mulholland, Lauren Gomez, and Zoe Kaplan.

To my agent, Sarah Fuentes, for exemplifying—from our first life-changing email exchange to my least coherent phone call—what a truly trusting, symbiotic professional partnership looks like. Thank you for your unflinching support, your unshatterable integrity, and your whip-smart insights into people, prose, and processes alike.

To every Barnraisers Project participant and *White Pages* reader, for everything that I learned and continue to learn from you, for all the ways that you helped me feel less alone, and for collectively holding and supporting myself and my family financially. I was able to write this book both because of your wisdom and emotional support, and (on a practical level) a lattice of donations, contributions, and subscriptions from around the globe.

To Carly Ganz, my brilliant professional partner, for so many gifts. A quick aside: The unanswered question behind many books written by parents (particularly male parents) is, "Who provided the childcare that enabled you to write the book?" In my case, there are many answers to that question (thanks to all the friends and family members who have composed Ida and Olof's village), but foremost among them has been Carly. Due to the support of Barnraisers donors and *White Pages* readers, while writing this book I was able to hire Carly in a unique role that matches her special combination of strengths—she is both a half-time nanny for our kids (she is, quite literally, a hero and role model to both of my children) and half-time Operations Manager for Barnraisers. As part of her duties in that second half of her role, she was a key proofreader/consultant/confidante on multiple drafts of this manuscript. Carly, you are a treasure, and all four of us are better for your wisdom, care, and creativity. You have lived and breathed it alongside me and strengthened both this book and our family in innumerable ways.

To Sarah Wheeler and Courtney Martin, for being the world's best art friends and my first glimpse into what a beloved community with other writers could look like (while also consistently writing sentences and paragraphs that just absolutely shatter me).

To Anne Helen Petersen, for being the most generous, curious, and openhearted writer that I have ever encountered. Not only did your interest in my work and ideas set up the dominos that would eventually lead to this book, but the way you model delight and critical wonder about ideas and people alike has been a constant source of inspiration.

To Lyz Lenz, the absolute best in the Midwest, and our entire shared *Flyover Politics* community (as well as the *White Pages* weekly discussion gang). I have grown (both as a writer and a human being) in immeasurable ways both thanks to your unflinching/heartbreaking/hilarious writing and the warmhearted, cage-rattling community of weirdos with whom both of us get to interact each day.

To Christy Hays and her merry band of artists, miscreants, and community builders in Butte, for both running the best damn writing residency in America (Dear Butte, of course) and for showing me, in practice, what caring about place and people looks like (and a special thanks to Kathleen Maclaughlin, one of America's best writers about class and inequity, for a pretty unbeatable Butte tour).

To a lifetime of friends—from Clancy to Milwaukee—who loved me at so many stages of the journey depicted on these pages. If you are reading this and wondering "I remember Garrett in that moment—I wonder if our relationship was/is meaningful to him?" The answer is yes.

To Jake Lessem, Casey Parks, and Athena Palmer, for the million reasons that you were the first friends I thought to call when I found out I would get to write this book.

To Milwaukee Public Schools and the Milwaukee Friends Meeting for providing such caring homes for Kjersti, Olof, Ida, and me.

To Lucinda Williams, the cast and crew of the television program *The Bear,* and Noboru Nakamura (the designer of the Ikea Poäng armchair), for their foundational contributions to my writing process.

To the city of Missoula, Montana, a place that technically has a population of 80,000 but is somehow home to at least 500,000 writers.

To Eric, Colin, Brian, Nate, and Anna (as well as your partners and my much beloved, nibling nephews and nieces) for making "fifth Bucks child" my proudest identity.

To Mum and Dad, for everything I've tried to reflect in these pages (and so much more). Being your son is the greatest gift imaginable.

And finally, to Kjersti, Olof, and Ida, for the loudest laughs, the happiest tears, the most soulful sighs, the deepest pearls of wisdom, and the warmest hugs. I love each of you more than I will ever be able to express.

About the Author

Garrett Bucks grew up in a number of places, but especially Montana. He is the founder of The Barnraisers Project and the author of *The White Pages* newsletter. He currently lives in Milwaukee, Wisconsin, with his wife and two children. *The Right Kind of White* is his first book. To learn more about his work, writing, and events, visit https://garrettbucks.com.